BROUGHT TO YOU BY

SUPERKID ACADEMY

A SIMPLE GUIDE FOR HOME USE

THE FRUIT OF THE SPIRIT IN YOU

BIBLE STUDY FOR KIDS!

Ordinary kids doing extraordinary things through the power of God's Word!

TABLE OF CONTENTS

WELCOME!

Dear Parent/Teacher,

I believe you will experience great and exciting things as you begin the faith adventure of *Superkid Academy Home Bible Study for Kids—The Fruit of the Spirit in You.*

As you launch into this faith-building time with your family or small group, take the opportunity to seek the Lord's direction about how to minister these lessons for maximum impact. God's Word does not return to Him void, and He will see to it that your children are BLESSED and grow strong in faith as you step out in His Anointing to teach them about Him.

Please keep in mind that we are praying for you. We believe and release our faith for a powerful anointing on you as you teach and impart His wisdom, and that your Superkids are strong in the Lord and mighty for Him.

Remember, we here at Academy Headquarters want to be a resource for you. Make sure you are in our contact base so we can keep in touch. And, let us know how we can better serve you and your Superkids.

We love you and look forward to hearing from you!

Love,

Commander Kellie

Commander Kellie

ACKNOWLEDGMENTS

I am so excited that Superkid Academy is making a difference in the hearts of kids all over the world! God is faithful to complete what He starts and, with His help, we have seen the extraordinary in the lives of countless children and families.

I would first like to thank the Lord who called and equipped me to minister to children. Part of that equipping has been through the support of my family. My husband, Steve, has been such an encourager and sounding board as this project has progressed. Thank you, Steve, for your patience, prayer, love and support—especially through the late nights. I love you!

I'm not sure whether motherhood made me a better children's minister or vice versa—all I know is that through the years, they meshed together. The result was a family of kids who helped me and ministered beside me, pouring their own hearts and energy into the Superkids. Thank you Rachel, Lyndsey, Jenny, Max and Emily for making this an all-family ministry. You make it fun!

Partnership is such a vital part of successful children's ministry. We trust God as our Source, and partner with each other to walk out His plan for our lives. I also want to thank the people whose faithfulness has made Superkid Academy fruitful all these years:

Commanders Dana and Linda Johnson—Your friendship and love mean more to me than you know. Thank you for making Superkid Academy a REAL place!

Kim Stephenson—My partner and covenant friend in ministry. I wouldn't want to do this without you, and I'm thankful I don't have to!

Jenni Drennen—You have the God-given, genius ability to "get it done" all while keeping the commanders in line and happy. You are simply wonderful!

Lyndsey Swisher—Your ability to creatively communicate the heart of Superkid Academy through writing, directing film and teaching is truly amazing. What a daughter! I love you with all my heart.

Our team at KCM—especially John Copeland and James Tito, for "biting the bullet" and declaring, "We're doing this!" And then, doing it with excellence. Thank you to our other team members who have worked so hard to make this Superkid Academy Curriculum right: Heather Main, Christine Schuelke and Katelyn Kurth—thank you for dedicating countless hours to it. Thank you, Cindy Hames and your department and Carleen Higgins in TV. Let's do it again!

Very importantly, I want to thank Pastors George and Terri Pearsons and the EMIC children's team. You believed and sowed and prayed and made Superkid Academy into a real place with real Superkids. I'll never forget it, and Jesus won't either.

And, to the hundreds of real Superkids at Eagle Mountain International Church and now all over the world, thank you! And remember, once a Superkid, always a Superkid!

Last but not least, I am deeply grateful to my wonderful parents, Kenneth and Gloria Copeland, for instilling in me the life of faith, for giving me the uncompromised Word to pass on to the Superkids, and for being absolutely, firmly and predictably dedicated to the Word of God. I love being your daughter!

I love you all!

Commander Kellie

Commander Kellie

LEADING YOUR SUPERKID ACADEMY:
A SIMPLE GUIDE FOR HOME USE

We are excited that you have brought Superkid Academy into your living room with the Home Bible Study for Kids! This powerful, Bible-based curriculum will guide your children into building a strong, personal relationship with the Lord and inspire them to live an extraordinary, faith-filled life.

Each of the 13 weeks included in this study provide five days of lessons, including a:

- **Lesson Introduction From Commander Kellie:** As the creator of Superkid Academy with more than 20 years' experience ministering to children, Kellie Copeland Swisher has a unique anointing and perspective for reaching children with the uncompromised Word of God. She passes on her wisdom through these timeless segments.
- **Lesson Outline:** Each lesson contains three main points, subpoints and supporting scriptures to empower you to clearly communicate the truth to your children.
- **Memory Verse:** Throughout the week, your kids will have the opportunity to memorize and understand a scripture. More than that, they'll learn how to apply it directly to their lives.
- **Bible Lesson:** Each Bible Lesson reinforces the memory verse and the principle behind it. Discussion questions will help you lead your children through not only comprehending the passage of scripture, but also giving it meaning in their lives.
- **Giving Lesson:** Each week, you will have the opportunity to teach your children about the importance of tithing and giving so they can be "blessed to be a blessing" in the Body of Christ.
- **Game Time:** Reinforces the message and gives families an occasion to celebrate what they've learned in a fun way.
- **Activity Page:** Reinforces the lesson through acrostics, word searches, mazes and other puzzles.
- **Supplements:** Support the memory verse and lesson—two will be provided each week, including:
  - **Object Lesson:** Illustrates the focus of the lesson and provides visual and hands-on elements to the teaching.
  - **Real Deal:** Highlights a historical person, place or event that illustrates the current lesson's theme.
  - **Storybook Theater:** Reinforces the message with creative, read-aloud stories.
  - **Food Fun:** Takes you and your children into the kitchen where you will discuss, illustrate and experience God's truth, using everyday items.
  - **Academy Lab:** Brings the lesson and science together.

And, don't forget the enclosed Praise and Worship CD! These original, upbeat, kid-friendly songs put the Word in your children's minds and hearts. The CD can be listened to around the house or in the car, and the karaoke, sing-along tracks allow your kids to sing their favorite songs.

Making the Curriculum Work for Your Family

Superkid Academy's Home Bible Study for Kids gives you the flexibility to teach your children in a way that works for you. Each week's lesson is divided into five days of teaching. However, we understand that no two families—or their schedules—are the same, so feel free to adjust the lessons to meet your needs. Use all five days of lessons or select only a few to cover each week. Whether you're using the curriculum as part of your home school, as a boost to your family devotions or in a weekly small group, you have the flexibility to make it work for you.

A Homeschool Bible Curriculum

Superkid Academy's Home Bible Study for Kids is easy to use, flexible and interactive—no dry Bible lessons here! It is ideal for a variety of learning styles. Each of the 13 weeks contains five days of lessons—one Bible Lesson, one Giving Lesson, one Game Time and two other lessons or stories to support the week's message. You may choose to use all five days of lessons or pick and choose the ones that work best for your educational structure. Optional variations for several of the lessons have been included to meet a variety of needs.

Each week's Snapshot provides the major points of the lesson, the memory verse and a list of supplies needed for that week, allowing you to easily prepare and customize each week's lessons. Here are just a few additional ideas for customizing for your home school:

- Re-read the Bible passage each day throughout the week to give your children—and you—time to meditate on the high-lighted scripture
- Use one or more of the discussion questions as a journaling exercise
- Begin a weekly, family Game Night
- Use the Storybook Theater in your nighttime read-aloud routine

Family Devotions

Superkid Academy's Home Bible Study for Kids empowers you to disciple your children and teach them the Word of God in an easy, fun way. You may choose to use all five days' worth of lessons, or select only a few. Each lesson takes less than 15 minutes, so the curriculum fits easily into your busy life.

Lessons are numbered 1-5, giving you the flexibility to include whichever lesson fits your daily schedule for that week. This allows you freedom to plan around work schedules, church commitments and extracurricular activities. Here are two sample schedules:

5-Day Schedule

Sunday—Church (no lesson)

Monday—Bible Lesson

Tuesday—Object Lesson

Wednesday—Midweek services (no lesson)

Thursday—Giving Lesson

Friday—Storybook Theater

Saturday—Game Time

3-Day Schedule

Sunday—Church (no lesson)

Monday— Bible Lesson

Tuesday—Soccer practice (no lesson)

Wednesday—Giving Lesson

Thursday—Soccer practice (no lesson)

Friday—Object Lesson

Saturday—Family time (no lesson)

A Weekly Small Group

Superkid Academy's Home Bible Study for Kids is designed for use over several days, but a week's worth of lessons can easily be consolidated for a small group. Simply choose the lessons that work best for your location and schedule and allow additional time for discussion and prayer.

Sample Small Group Schedule:

6 p.m.	Bible Lesson with discussion time
6:30 p.m.	Giving Lesson
6:45 p.m.	Object Lesson and prayer time
7:15 p.m.	Game Time
7:45 p.m.	Refreshments
8 p.m.	Closing

Thank you again for implementing Superkid Academy's Home Bible Study for Kids. We stand with you in faith as you disciple your children in the things that matter to Him. Proverbs 22:6 *(KJV)* says, "Train up a child in the way he should go: and when he is old, he will not depart from it." At Superkid Academy, we are confident that God will bless your efforts, and that you and your children will see the reality of THE BLESSING in all you do (Numbers 6:24-26).

Love,

Commander Kellie

Commander Kellie

HEALTH & SAFETY DISCLAIMER FOR "SUPERKID ACADEMY CURRICULUM"

Superkid Academy is a ministry of Eagle Mountain International Church, aka Kenneth Copeland Ministries (hereafter "EMIC"). The "Superkid Academy Curriculum" (hereafter "SKA Curriculum") provides age-appropriate teaching material to be used in the religious instruction of children. The SKA Curriculum includes physical activities in which children and leaders may participate. Before engaging in any of the physical activities, participants should be in good physical condition as determined by their health care provider. EMIC is not responsible for injuries resulting from the implementation of activities suggested within the SKA Curriculum. Prior to implementing the SKA Curriculum, carefully review your organization's safety and health policies, and determine whether the SKA Curriculum is appropriate for your organization's intended use.

By purchasing the SKA Curriculum, I, individually and/or as authorized representative for my organization, hereby agree to release, defend, hold harmless, and covenant not to sue EMIC, its officers, deacons, ministers, directors, employees, volunteers, contractors, staff, affiliates, agents and attorneys (collectively, the "EMIC Parties"), and the property of EMIC for any claim, including claims for negligence and gross negligence of any one or more of the EMIC Parties, arising out of my use or organization's use of and participation in the SKA Curriculum, participation in the suggested activities contained within the SKA Curriculum, or resulting from first-aid treatment or services rendered as a result of or in connection with the activities or participation in the activities.

WEEK 1: TASTE AND SEE

 Memory Verse: *Taste and see that the Lord is good. Oh, the joys of those who take refuge in him!*
—Psalm 34:8

WEEK 1: SNAPSHOT

TASTE AND SEE

DAY	TYPE OF LESSON	LESSON TITLE	SUPPLIES
Day 1	Bible Lesson	Israel and the Golden Calf	None
Day 2	Read-Aloud	Superkid Academy Worldwide: Germany	Images of Germany (Rhine River, Daniel Gabriel Fahrenheit, Heinrich Geissler, castles, Neuschwanstein Castle, Bavaria, Berlin, Brandenburg Gate, Cologne Cathedral, countryside, etc.)
Day 3	Giving Lesson	God's Partner	1 Set of interlocking plastic blocks or other toy building blocks, 1 Table
Day 4	Food Fun	Big Buckaroo Burger	Microwave oven, Microwave-safe plate, Potholder, Paper towels, Knife, Grill or pan to cook burgers, Hamburger patties (1 for each family member), 2 Pieces of bacon per burger, Mushrooms (sautéed), 1 Can of french-fried onion rings, 1 Slice of cheddar cheese per burger, Barbecue sauce, 2 Slices of Texas toast (extra thick bread, toasted on 1 side) per burger, Butter
Day 5	Game Time	Sandwich Cookie Whiteout	1 Table, 2 Packages of cream-filled sandwich cookies, 2 Plates, Upbeat music (optional)
Bonus	Activity Page	The Goodness Connection	1 Copy for each child

Lesson Introduction:

Our God is good!

We must be convinced of that fact, and we must communicate it to our children. God's goodness is the very first truth that Satan lied about and perverted in the Garden of Eden, and he still attempts to dim the importance of that truth today.

It's important for us—and our children—to accept God's goodness because the Word tells us that when we taste the Lord's goodness, we walk in THE BLESSING (Psalm 34:8). Our children will acquire a taste for the things of God if we make sure that God's goodness is communicated to them.

The easiest way to demonstrate God's goodness is this: Make sure you treat your children well so that you represent your heavenly Father well. Your children will see God and make decisions about Him based on the example set by you and other leaders in their lives (ex: pastors, teachers, coaches, friends' parents, etc.). Let your children taste how sweet God can be, and watch The Sweet Life become their life!

Love,

Commander Dana

Commander Dana

Lesson Outline:

This week your children will learn about God's goodness. Before you dive into teaching them about the fruit of the spirit, first help them understand how good and loving their heavenly Father is. If they want all that God has for them, aka "The Sweet Life," then they must do a couple of things: 1) Get rid of evil behavior and 2) Hunger for God's Word.

This week, begin to share these points with your children. Discuss them as you complete this week's lessons and even in your everyday conversations.

I. GOD WANTS US TO TASTE AND SEE HOW GOOD HE IS

a. The word *taste* means to "perceive, or recognize."

b. Developing a taste for God's Word requires more than one daily "meal." Joshua 1:8

c. Trusting in God's goodness brings "THE BLESSING." Psalm 34:8

II. GET RID OF ALL EVIL BEHAVIOR 1 Peter 2:1

a. Ungodly living messes up our ability to taste the good things of God.

b. Worldly things leave a bad taste in our hearts, and a wrong memory in our minds.

c. "The Sweet Life" lets us taste God's goodness every day! Psalm 119:103

III. SUPERKIDS WHO HUNGER FOR GOD'S WORD GROW STRONG 1 Peter 2:2-3

a. The good things of God are like an awesome meal for our spirits.

b. After we taste something really good, we tell our friends how good it is!

c. The more of our heavenly Father we "taste and see," the hungrier we get!

Notes:_____

_____

_____

_____

_____

_____

_____

_____

DAY 1: BIBLE LESSON

ISRAEL AND THE GOLDEN CALF

Memory Verse: *Taste and see that the Lord is good. Oh, the joys of those who take refuge in him!*
—Psalm 34:8

(Corresponds with Lesson Outline No. II)

Even after the Lord freed them from slavery in Egypt, the children of Israel doubted Him and created a false idol in His place. This passage is a great reminder of how far we can move away from God when left to our own devices. God desires that we follow Him faithfully and remember The Sweet Life He has given us through His Son, Jesus.

Read Exodus 32:1-26, 29:
The Golden Calf

When the people saw how long it was taking Moses to come back down the mountain, they gathered around Aaron. "Come on," they said, "make us some gods who can lead us. We don't know what happened to this fellow Moses, who brought us here from the land of Egypt."

So Aaron said, "Take the gold rings from the ears of your wives and sons and daughters, and bring them to me."

All the people took the gold rings from their ears and brought them to Aaron. Then Aaron took the gold, melted it down, and molded it into the shape of a calf. When the people saw it, they exclaimed, "O Israel, these are the gods who brought you out of the land of Egypt!"

Aaron saw how excited the people were, so he built an altar in front of the calf. Then he announced, "Tomorrow will be a festival to the Lord!"

The people got up early the next morning to sacrifice burnt offerings and peace offerings. After this, they celebrated with feasting and drinking, and they indulged in pagan revelry.

The Lord told Moses, "Quick! Go down the mountain! Your people whom you brought from the land of Egypt have corrupted themselves. How quickly they have turned away from the way I commanded them to live! They have melted down gold and made a calf, and they have bowed down and sacrificed to it. They are saying, 'These are your gods, O Israel, who brought you out of the land of Egypt.'"

Then the Lord said, "I have seen how stubborn and rebellious these people are. Now leave me alone so my fierce anger can blaze against them, and I will destroy them. Then I will make you, Moses, into a great nation."

But Moses tried to pacify the Lord his God. "O Lord!" he said. "Why are you so angry with your own people whom you brought from the land of Egypt with such great power and such a strong hand? Why let the Egyptians say, 'Their God rescued them with the evil intention of slaughtering them in the mountains and wiping them from the face of the earth'? Turn away from your fierce anger. Change your mind about this terrible disaster you have threatened against your people! Remember your servants Abraham, Isaac, and Jacob. You bound yourself with an oath to them, saying, 'I will make your descendants as numerous as the stars of heaven. And I will give them all of this land that I have promised to your descendants, and they will possess it forever.'"

So the Lord changed his mind about the terrible disaster he had threatened to bring on his people.

Then Moses turned and went down the mountain. He held in his hands the two stone tablets inscribed with the terms of the covenant. They were inscribed on both sides, front and back. These tablets were God's work; the words on them were written by God himself.

When Joshua heard the boisterous noise of the people shouting below them, he exclaimed to Moses, "It sounds like war in the camp!"

But Moses replied, "No, it's not a shout of victory nor the wailing of defeat. I hear the sound of a celebration."

When they came near the camp, Moses saw the calf and the dancing, and he burned with anger. He threw the stone tablets to the ground, smashing them at the foot of the mountain. He took the calf they had made and burned it. Then he ground it into powder, threw it into the water, and forced the people to drink it.

Finally, he turned to Aaron and demanded, "What did these people do to you to make you bring such terrible sin upon them?"

"Don't get so upset, my lord," Aaron replied. "You yourself know how evil these people are. They said to me, 'Make us gods who will lead us. We don't know what happened to this fellow Moses, who brought us here from the land of Egypt.' So I told them, 'Whoever has gold jewelry, take it off.' When they brought it to me, I simply threw it into the fire—and out came this calf!"

Moses saw that Aaron had let the people get completely out of control, much to the amusement of their enemies. So he stood at the entrance to the camp and shouted, "All of you who are on the Lord's side, come here and join me." And all the Levites gathered around him....

Then Moses told the Levites, "Today you have ordained yourselves for the service of the Lord…you have earned a blessing."

Discussion Questions:

1. **What are three things that happened in this passage?**

   Answers will vary, but make sure your children understand the passage.

2. **Why was God so angry that the Israelites had created a golden calf to worship?**

   God is the One, true God. He won't share His people with any other so-called "gods" that are really just representations of His enemy, Satan. God wants us to taste and see (to perceive and recognize) how good He is and that ungodly living messes up our ability to taste the good things of God. He wants so much to BLESS His people and give them "The Sweet Life" that's only available in Him! (See Lesson Outline No. I a-c, II a)

3. **From what had God just delivered the children of Israel? Why?**

   He had just delivered them from slavery in Egypt. They were His people, and He loved them. He wanted to give them a better life.

4. **Why do you think the people forgot what God had done for them?**

   There are several possible answers. Perhaps:

- They became distracted because Moses had been gone so long up on the mountain.

- They doubted God from the beginning.

- They wanted to have some "thing" to worship—something they could see—as opposed to their unseen, yet very real, God.

5. Read Hebrews 9:13-15:

Under the old system, the blood of goats and bulls and the ashes of a young cow could cleanse people's bodies from ceremonial impurity. Just think how much more the blood of Christ will purify our consciences from sinful deeds so that we can worship the living God. For by the power of the eternal Spirit, Christ offered himself to God as a perfect sacrifice for our sins. That is why he is the one who mediates a new covenant between God and people, so that all who are called can receive the eternal inheritance God has promised them. For Christ died to set them free from the penalty of the sins they had committed under that first covenant.

6. How does this passage relate to what we read in this lesson?

When the Israelites sinned, they had to make atonement—"pay" for it—with the blood of an innocent animal. This was a picture of Jesus, who was to come, the sinless, innocent Lamb of God, whose blood was to be shed to pay for our sins. Under the new covenant, Jesus became the perfect sacrifice. His perfect blood was shed once and for all to pay for every sin—past, present and future. When we sin, we need to repent (turn away from it), ask God to forgive us, receive our forgiveness by faith, and then rejoice that Jesus' blood washes us from it forever (1 John 1:9)!

(Parents, make sure your children understand that they don't need to live in fear that God is mad at them or going to punish or harm them when they make mistakes. He loves them (John 17:23). Jesus took mankind's punishment for sin so we could go free and be restored to the sweet fellowship God created us to have with our heavenly Father like Adam and Eve had in the Garden of Eden and Jesus has with the Father.)

7. How can we apply what we have learned from this passage to our own lives?

We should never forget all the good things—The Sweet Life—God has given us. We shouldn't let anything become more important or distract us from Him. Ungodly living messes up our ability to taste the good things of God. (See Lesson Outline No. II a)

Notes:_____

_____

_____

_____

_____

_____

_____

_____

_____

_____

DAY 2: READ-ALOUD | **SUPERKID ACADEMY WORLDWIDE: GERMANY**

 Suggested Time: 15 minutes

 Key Scripture: Therefore, if anyone is in Christ, he is a new creation; old things have passed away; behold, all things have become new. —2 Corinthians 5:17 NKJV

Supplies: ☐ Images of Germany (Rhine River, Daniel Gabriel Fahrenheit, Heinrich Geissler, castles, Neuschwanstein Castle, Bavaria, Berlin, Brandenburg Gate, Cologne Cathedral, countryside, etc.)

(Corresponds with Lesson Outline No. I, III)

Background:

In this version of the *Superkid Academy Home Bible Study,* we launch a new series, **Superkid Academy Worldwide**, exploring countries and people groups across the vast expanse of our planet. We will zoom in on fascinating aspects of culture and history, and most importantly, focus on how God is working within the hearts of people and transforming the places where they live.

Today, we explore Germany and follow our brave, and occasionally bumbling, news reporter, Steve Storyberg, as he explores the wonders of Germany, and meets two children who illustrate how God is working in the hearts of Superkids everywhere.

Story:

Our story begins with a roving reporter and his film crew. They're standing with a TV camera and equipment, nestled in the German countryside, surrounded by colorful trees and a small village. Birds are chirping, and a duck swims down a trickling river, as Steve's crew prepares to go LIVE:

"Steve, it's coming to *you* in 30 seconds," says Kathleen Connery, a smart-looking lady dressed in black, wearing headphones, holding a clipboard and looking intently at newsman Steve Storyberg.

"Ready to rock, roll and report!" says Steve, with a wink as he adjusts his microphone. Steve's red tie and dark suit stand out against the greens of the trees and bushes, his hair blowing a little in the breeze.

"Sound check!" calls out soundman George Lupas, looking down at his equipment while waiting for Steve's check.

"Let's see…. Wow, I sure am hungry! I wish I had a bologna and cheese sandwich," says Steve. Realizing that his friends are not laughing, he quickly continues. "I mean, testing one, two, three!"

"Good to go," George replies, giving a thumbs up.

Steve looks at the camera as the words appear across the teleprompter screen mounted in front of the lens. Kathleen points at him, indicating he's on, but Steve freezes. The lettering on the screen looks blurry, and

Steve suddenly realizes he left his glasses in his briefcase. But it's too late.

"Hello, I'm Steve Storyberg, and this is Superkid Academy Worldwide News, coming to you super LIVE from the super country of Germany!"

Steve squints, trying to read the teleprompter. Kathleen looks puzzled. But Steve pushes ahead. He has to. It's LIVE.

"Uh, this grape county…"

Alarmed, Kathleen mouths the words, "Great country."

"This great country is home for many amusing…"

"Amazing," whispers Kathleen.

"Amazing inventions. Inventions like…." Steve suddenly stares at Kathleen, who is holding out his glasses right in front of his face.

"Your glasses!" she says in a loud whisper. Steve smiles and puts them on.

"Inventions like…my glasses! I mean, inventions like movable type, invented by Johannes Gutenberg, who gave us the very first printed Bible in 1456."

Kathleen, George and cameraman Harrison Borg breathe a sigh of relief, all at the same time. Steve now continues with confidence…

"And how would we know exactly how cold or hot it is, if Daniel Gabriel Fahrenheit, a Dutch-German-Polish scientist, engineer and glass blower hadn't invented the thermometer? And what about Heinrich Geissler? He invented fluorescent lighting, helping us all to see the light! And, if you want to see the sights, the spectacular Neuschwanstein Castle nestled in Bavaria in the beautiful, snowy Alps, is a great place to start. Or, you could visit the famous Brandenburg Gate in Berlin and the Cologne Cathedral, the third tallest cathedral in the world that took over 600 years to build!"[1]

A duck quacks in the distance.

"And what about sauerkraut?" Steve continues.

Kathleen and George glance at each other with confused looks as Steve departs from the script…again.

"That's right, sauerkraut, which I happen to love, with a nice fat hot dog. Ya' know, sauerkraut is actually finely cut cabbage with a strong, sour flavor that forms when bacteria ferments the sugars in the…"

Steve's lecture about sour cabbage is cut short when a group of excited children run past him, weaving in and out of the camera equipment, but being careful not to disturb anything. They brush by the surprised newsman and scamper over a wooden bridge, heading for an old-fashioned church across a grassy field.

"Wow, these kids must love sauerkraut as much as I do, folks!"

Kathleen points to the teleprompter, urging Steve to get back to the script. But then, something else happens. Two of the children stop, turn around and walk back toward Steve.

"Looks like I may get a super, LIVE interview, right here on the spot, ladies and gentlemen…well, hello there!"

---

1   "Cologne Cathedral," http://www.colognecathedral.net

The boy and girl look at Steve with blank expressions.

"Oh, wait, I know a little German. Good day! I mean, *Guten tag!*"

The children smile.

Steve fumbles with the mic, hitting it against his forehead, trying to think of more phrases. He begins counting in German, *"Ein, zwei, drei…"*

"Hi Steve," the girl says, grinning. "We like your show. I'm Arnelle, and this is Bertram. We're going to our new kids' church. It's really fun. Come and join us."

Steve, rarely at a loss for words, is at a loss for words. "Uh, well, thank you, but I, well, I don't know, uh, I…"

Suddenly, Kathleen steps in to rescue him, once again. Without her headphones and clipboard, and holding her own microphone, the seasoned newswoman takes over.

"Thank you, Steve. It's clear to see that these children are part of something wonderful here in Germany, a church service just for kids. I can imagine it's filled with stories and games, and probably some great snacks!"

"Speaking of tasty snacks," begins Steve. But Kathleen jumps back in.

"American missionaries established this kids' church program, and the results have been…"[2]

Now Steve jumps in. "Absolutely super! From what Bertram just told me, there are more than 40 children in his church now, whereas before, counting himself and Arnelle, there were only around seven. Very impressive!"

"Steve, you can see the excitement in their faces. You just know they're learning more and more about Jesus, and how to live their lives for Him. And, they're not afraid to tell their friends, even inviting newsmen they find on the way to church. How 'bout that?"

"Well, right, that's nice," Steve adds, "but I think I'm a little too big to go to…"

"You can come as our guest," says Bertram. "They have church for adults, too. Come on, let's go! You'll love it, Steve!"

They grab his hands and pull hard. Kathleen takes his mic.

"I'm Steve Storyberg, for Superkid Academy Worldwide News," he says, almost stumbling over the wooden planks on the bridge, and struggling to keep up with them. "Say, I'm, uh, kinda hungry," Steve blurts out. "I don't suppose you have hot dogs…with ketchup…and sauerkraut?"

"It's sauerkraut Saturday," says Arnelle, "in your honor!"

"And there you have it, ladies and gentlemen," Kathleen says, wrapping it up. "God is doing great things here in Germany, and all around the world."

The duck quacks again.

"And from the look of things, I'd say everybody is happy. Filling in for Steve Sauerkraut—I mean, Storyberg—I'm Kathleen Connery, Superkid Academy Worldwide News."

---

2   "Western Europe-Germany-Doris Kühn–A Children's Ministry Transformed," *Willow Creek Association, Global Leadership Summit* - International Stories, willowcreek.com/about/story.asp (7/10/2013).

Discussion Questions:

1. What did you learn about German inventions in this story?

2. What did you learn about how God is moving in Germany?

3. Tell about a time when you invited a friend to church.

4. If someone asked you to pray for children in Germany, what would you pray?

5. Have you ever tasted German food? Explain what you ate, where you ate it and what you thought of it!

Variation No. 1: Writing Assignment

For older children, assign a 1-2 page paper on Germany and what God is doing there. Have your children include:

- Key information about Germany

- Significant ministry outreaches happening within Germany and/or coming out of Germany to the rest of the world

- Famous Christian leaders and inventors from Germany

- Your children's recommendations for reaching the lost in Germany

Variation No. 2: Map Skills

Print a blank map of Germany from the Internet. Have your children mark the capital (Berlin), other large cities, major rivers, bordering countries and neighboring bodies of water. Ask them to trace the map several times throughout the week to help them remember and gain better understanding of Germany.

Variation No. 3: International Food

Visit a German restaurant or serve strudel one evening for dessert.

Notes:_____

_____

_____

_____

_____

_____

_____

_____

_____

_____

DAY 3: GIVING LESSON | GOD'S PARTNER

Suggested Time: 10 minutes

Offering Scripture: [I thank my God] for your fellowship (your sympathetic cooperation and contributions and partnership) in advancing the good news.... –Philippians 1:5 AMP

Supplies: ■ 1 Set of interlocking plastic blocks or other toy building blocks, ■ 1 Table

(Corresponds with Lesson Outline No. I, III b)

Prior to Lesson:

Display the building blocks or interlocking plastic blocks on a table. Allow children to assist with the demonstration. They must work together, as a team, building a tower with the blocks.

Lesson Instructions:

Today, you will be working together to build a tower using the building blocks on the table. Let's see just how well you can build it!

As you build the tower, I'll read the giving scripture from Philippians 1:5 AMP. It says, "[I thank my God] for your fellowship (your sympathetic cooperation and contributions and partnership) in advancing the good news...." When we tell others the good news about Jesus, we are sharing about how good God is. We share with others how trusting in God's goodness brings THE BLESSING. After they taste how good He is, they'll want to tell their friends, too!

Just like you are working together, partnering with one another to build this tower, the Apostle Paul needed partners to help him share the good news of Jesus. Paul's partners believed in the power of spreading God's Word around the world and gave offerings to support his mission.

Let's see your progress. It's amazing what can be accomplished when people work together! Did you know the Lord still needs partners just like He did back when Paul was alive? That's right, and we can be those partners. You may be thinking, *How can I be a partner with God, I'm just a kid?* When we bring our offerings to God, we are partnering with Him, and allowing the gospel to be shared around the world. Let's prepare our offerings for this week's service so we can honor God with our giving.

Notes:_____

_____

_____

_____

_____

DAY 4: FOOD FUN · BIG BUCKAROO BURGER

Suggested Time: 10 minutes

Memory Verse: Taste and see that the Lord is good. Oh, the joys of those who take refuge in him! —Psalm 34:8

Recipe:

Ingredients: ☐ Hamburger patties (1 for each family member), ☐ 2 Pieces of bacon per burger, ☐ Mushrooms, sautéed, ☐ 1 Can of french-fried onion rings, ☐ 1 Slice of cheddar cheese per burger, ☐ Barbecue sauce, ☐ 2 Slices of Texas toast (extra-thick bread, toasted on 1 side) per burger, ☐ Butter

1. Season the hamburger patty with a little salt and pepper as desired. Grill or cook in a pan on the stove. Cover the hamburger with foil to prevent the meat from drying out until it's time to assemble the burger.

2. Cook bacon until crispy. Drain on paper towels and set aside.

3. Sauté thinly sliced mushrooms in a small amount of butter.

4. Place the hamburger patty on a microwave oven-safe plate; top with mushrooms and bacon. Place a cheddar cheese slice over the top and heat in the microwave oven until the cheese has melted. Remove the plate from the microwave using a potholder.

5. Prepare the bread by spreading barbecue sauce on the toasted side of the bread; enough to make it juicy, but not too much because it will make the bread soggy.

6. Place the hamburger patty on 1 piece of bread. Top the patty with onion rings. Place the "lid," or other piece of bread, on the burger. Cut the burger in half, if desired, to make it easier to eat.

Supplies: ■ Microwave oven, ■ Microwave-safe plate, ■ Potholder, ■ Paper towels, ■ Knife, ■ Grill or pan to cook burgers, ■ Hamburger patties (1 for each family member), ■ 2 Pieces of bacon per burger, ■ Mushrooms, sautéed, ■ 1 Can of french-fried onion rings, ■ 1 Slice of cheddar cheese per burger, ■ Barbecue sauce, ■ 2 Slices of Texas toast (extra thick bread, toasted on 1 side) per burger, ■ Butter

(Corresponds with Lesson Outline No. I, III)

Prior to Lesson:

This is an excellent lesson to do during dinner when the whole family is present. Allow your children to help with the meal preparations so they can get even more excited about eating what they've made. Allow your children to mold and season the hamburger patties, cook the bacon, mushrooms and toast, following the recipe above.

Lesson Instructions:

Today, we're making an "all-American" favorite dish: the hamburger. This is not just *any* hamburger, this is a "Big Buckaroo Burger"!

First of all, we'll take this nice, juicy hamburger patty and top it with a spoonful of yummy, sautéed mushrooms and a crispy piece of bacon. Now, let's cover it with a slice of delicious cheddar cheese. The next step is to pop it into the microwave oven until the cheese is nice and melted and the hamburger patty is nice and hot. For safety, we'll use a potholder to remove the plate from the microwave oven. Boy, does that smell good! Mmmmm!

It's time to complete the "Big Buckaroo Burger": Let's take two pieces of Texas toast and lay them on a clean plate.

Would you like barbecue sauce on your hamburger? If your answer is yes, then let's spread some barbecue sauce on each piece of Texas toast, but not too much because no one enjoys a soggy burger! OK, time to put the "Big Buckaroo Burger" together: Place the hamburger patty on one piece of Texas toast, pile it high with some onion rings, and then put the "lid" (other slice of toast) on top. Now, the best part—eating it!

Serve the hamburger, but tell children not to eat it until you instruct them to do so.

Would you like to take a bite of your "Big Buckaroo Burger"? Is it possible to know how delicious this burger really is just by hearing a description of how good it tastes? It would be best to taste the hamburger yourself to really know how good it is, right? Well that's exactly what Psalm 34:8 tells us about God. This verse says, "Taste and see that the Lord is good. Oh, the joys of those who take refuge in him!" This scripture doesn't mean we need to take a big bite out of God! But the Bible is telling us that we shouldn't just stand around and watch others experience how good God is. He wants us to get a "taste" for ourselves. He wants each of us to know how much He loves and cares about us. You could say it like this: "God wants us to do our own taste test!" The more of our heavenly Father's goodness we "taste and see," the hungrier we get for Him. And, the more we hunger for Him and His Word, the stronger we get!

Now, who's ready to "taste" how good God is?

Variation—*Bon Appétit:*

Allow this lesson to be a jumping-off point for your family. If hamburgers are not the best choice for your family, consider making another family favorite like veggie burgers or homemade pizza. As long as you make the point that God's goodness needs to be personally experienced, the choice of food is yours. *Bon appétit!*

Notes:_____

_____

_____

_____

_____

DAY 5: GAME TIME

SANDWICH COOKIE WHITEOUT

 Suggested Time: 10 minutes

 Memory Verse: Taste and see that the Lord is good. Oh, the joys of those who take refuge in him! —Psalm 34:8

Supplies: ☐ 1 Table, ☐ 2 Packages of cream-filled sandwich cookies, ☐ 2 Plates, ☐ Upbeat music to play during the game (optional)

(Corresponds with Lesson Outline No. I)

Prior to Game:

Place the plates on opposite sides of the table. Place 15 cookies on each plate. Choose 2 players to challenge each other in this game.

Game Instructions:

Players will challenge each other by twisting open the cookie and eating the filling from the middle of the sandwich cookie. The first player to eat the fillings from all 15 cookies is the whiteout winner!

Game Goal:

A fun activity that relates the goodness of God to enjoying a tasty treat!

Final Word:

Sandwich cookies sure are tasty, but God is even tastier! When we taste how good He is—how much He loves and cares for us—we want more of Him. Think I'm kidding? Check out Psalm 34:8: "Taste and see that the Lord is good. Oh, the joys of those who take refuge in him!"

Notes:_____

_____

_____

_____

_____

_____

ACTIVITY PAGE   THE GOODNESS CONNECTION

Memory Verse: Taste and see that the Lord is good. Oh, the joys of those who take refuge in him! —Psalm 34:8

(Corresponds with Lesson Outline No. I)

This week, you've learned about God's goodness. Read what the Bible says about His goodness in these scriptures. Insert the word "good" or "goodness" in the blanks in order to complete the verse correctly.

And we know that God causes everything to work together for the _____ of those who love God and are called according to his purpose for them. Romans 8:28

How great is the _____ you have stored up for those who fear you. You lavish it on those who come to you for protection, blessing them before the watching world. Psalm 31:19

Surely your _____ and unfailing love will pursue me all the days of my life, and I will live in the house of the Lord forever. Psalm 23:6

The Lord is _____ and does what is right; he shows the proper path to those who go astray. Psalm 25:8

The Lord is _____, a strong refuge when trouble comes. He is close to those who trust in him. Nahum 1:7

ANSWER KEY:

And we know that God causes everything to work together for the <u>good</u> of those who love God and are called according to his purpose for them. Romans 8:28

How great is the <u>goodness</u> you have stored up for those who fear you. You lavish it on those who come to you for protection, blessing them before the watching world. Psalm 31:19

Surely your <u>goodness</u> and unfailing love will pursue me all the days of my life, and I will live in the house of the Lord forever. Psalm 23:6

The Lord is <u>good</u> and does what is right; he shows the proper path to those who go astray. Psalm 25:8

The Lord is <u>good</u>, a strong refuge when trouble comes. He is close to those who trust in him. Nahum 1:7

Notes:_____

_____

_____

_____

_____

_____

_____

_____

_____

_____

_____

_____

_____

_____

_____

_____

_____

_____

_____

WEEK 2: LOVE: THAT'S WHO GOD IS

 Memory Verse: I have revealed you to them, and I will continue to do so. Then your love for me will be in them, and I will be in them. –John 17:26

WEEK 2: SNAPSHOT

LOVE: THAT'S WHO GOD IS

DAY	TYPE OF LESSON	LESSON TITLE	SUPPLIES
Day 1	Bible Lesson	Peter and the Beggar	None
Day 2	Read-Aloud	Superkid Academy Worldwide: South Africa	Images of South-African sites–Kruger National Park, "The Big Five" animal group (lion, African elephant, Cape buffalo, leopard, rhinoceros), a diamond or gold mine, South African cities (Durban, Johannesburg, Cape Town, etc.), people groups that live in South Africa
Day 3	Giving Lesson	The Price Is Right	A small amount of money (about $8 in coins and bills), 1 Loaf of sliced bread, 1 Jar of peanut butter, 1 Squeeze bottle of jelly, 3 Card-stock price cards, 3 Envelopes
Day 4	Object Lesson	Master Seed	5 Different fruit samples (ex: apple, orange, strawberry, cherry, kiwi or watermelon), 1 Container
Day 5	Game Time	Tower Stack	Set of stacking boxes, A timer (or stopwatch), Prize
Bonus	Activity Page	Peter and the Beggar Crossword	1 Copy for each child

Lesson Introduction:

It can be difficult for kids to walk in love. Not only are children naturally somewhat self-centered, but in today's culture, love has lost its true meaning. It has become so "feeling" based that there is no substance to it. If a Superkid can understand the difference between his/her own natural ability to love and the ability to rely on and extend God's very own love, then he/she can choose to walk in the God kind of love.

It is important to first establish the concept of God's love inside us. To accomplish this, I use the illustration of making a peanut butter sandwich with bread that has a lot of shape to it. A little peanut butter in the middle of the piece of bread isn't good enough. A *great* sandwich has it spread from hump to hump, corner to corner and side to side! That is "shed abroad"! It's the same with God's love. He has put His love—and capacity to love— inside us.

When it feels impossible to love someone, this tells us we aren't using *His* love, we're trying to do it on our own. When we choose *His* love, it will show on the outside!

Love,

Commander Kellie

Commander Kellie

Lesson Outline:

This week your children begin learning about the individual fruit of the spirit. Love is the first fruit listed, and it is so important because God is love (1 John 4:16). It's His nature. Help your children understand the importance of love this week. It is not merely a romantic emotion, but rather the very nature of God. When your children exhibit the love of God, they are sharing His greatness with the world. They are, in fact, acting as ambassadors for Him.

I. THE FRUIT OF THE SPIRIT IS GOD'S NATURE BORN IN US

a. "...The love of God is shed abroad in our hearts by the Holy Ghost which is given unto us." Romans 5:5 KJV

b. The same love God loves Jesus with is in us (John 17:26). We can love others with that amazing God-love!

c. It isn't fruit until it shows up on the outside for others to see.

II. GOD IS LOVE; IT IS HIS VERY NATURE 1 John 4:16

a. God's nature (the fruit of the spirit) will lie inactive in us until we use it. Action is required!

b. When we do things in our own (fleshly) power, the supernatural is missing.

c. Without God's love, we live like mere men. 1 Corinthians 3:3

III. THE FRUIT THAT NEVER FAILS

a. All the other fruit comes from and works by love, God's own nature.

b. When we choose to walk in the spirit, we will not fail.

c. Our human love is not good enough for hard situations but His love never fails! 1 Corinthians 13:8

Notes:_____

_____

_____

_____

_____

_____

_____

_____

_____

DAY 1: BIBLE LESSON — PETER AND THE BEGGAR

Memory Verse: I have revealed you to them, and I will continue to do so. Then your love for me will be in them, and I will be in them. —John 17:26

(Corresponds with Lesson Outline No. I-III)

Today's Bible lesson shows love and faith in action. When we act on our faith in God and share His love with others, powerful, life-changing things happen.

Read Acts 3:1-11:
Peter Heals a Crippled Beggar

Peter and John went to the Temple one afternoon to take part in the three o'clock prayer service. As they approached the Temple, a man lame from birth was being carried in. Each day he was put beside the Temple gate, the one called the Beautiful Gate, so he could beg from the people going into the Temple. When he saw Peter and John about to enter, he asked them for some money.

Peter and John looked at him intently, and Peter said, "Look at us!" The lame man looked at them eagerly, expecting some money. But Peter said, "I don't have any silver or gold for you. But I'll give you what I have. In the name of Jesus Christ the Nazarene, get up and walk!"

Then Peter took the lame man by the right hand and helped him up. And as he did, the man's feet and ankles were instantly healed and strengthened. He jumped up, stood on his feet, and began to walk! Then, walking, leaping, and praising God, he went into the Temple with them.

All the people saw him walking and heard him praising God. When they realized he was the lame beggar they had seen so often at the Beautiful Gate, they were absolutely astounded! They all rushed out in amazement to Solomon's Colonnade, where the man was holding tightly to Peter and John.

Discussion Questions:

1. **Tell me this story in your own words.**

   Answers will vary, but make sure your children understand the passage.

2. **What was this beggar's life like?**

   Friends and family took him daily and sat him down at the Beautiful Gate so he could beg for money. His life was very limited. He couldn't walk, move, work or do other things like other people.

3. **What did the lame beggar want from Peter and John?**

   He wanted money.

4. **What did Peter give him instead?**

Peter, by the power of the resurrected Jesus, healed the man so he could walk.

5. **How did the man respond to his healing?**

He was so excited, he was jumping up and down, praising God, and hugging Peter and John.

6. **How did Peter show the beggar the fruit of God's love?**

He could have walked right by the beggar just as other people were doing, but instead, Peter stopped and prayed for him to be healed in Jesus' Name.

7. **How can we show God's love—the fruit that never fails—to others this week?**

Answers will vary.

Notes:

DAY 2: READ-ALOUD

SUPERKID ACADEMY WORLDWIDE: SOUTH AFRICA

 Suggested Time: 15 minutes

 Key Scripture: Have I not commanded you? Be strong and of good courage; do not be afraid nor be dismayed, for the Lord your God is with you wherever you go. —Joshua 1:9 NKJV

Supplies: ■ Images of South-African sites—Kruger National Park, "The Big Five" animal group (lion, African elephant, Cape buffalo, leopard, rhinoceros), A diamond or gold mine, South-African cities (Durban, Johannesburg, Cape Town, etc.), People groups that live in South Africa

(Corresponds with Lesson Outline No. I)

Background:

This week, our Superkid Academy Worldwide read-aloud adventure flies us across the world to the huge continent of Africa and drops us down at the very southern tip of the country, in South Africa, a place of big cities, wide-open spaces and lots of lions in its national parks. And, a place that needs lionhearted Christians!

Story:

Superkid Academy Worldwide vans rumble along through the vast plains of South Africa, as big clouds of dust spread into the sky behind them.

Both vans are air-conditioned against the heat, and loaded with TV equipment and supplies. Steve Storyberg and Kathleen Connery ride in Van No.1, where the camera is LIVE as Steve speaks from the passenger seat:

"I'm Steve Storyberg, and this is Superkid Academy Worldwide News, coming to you super LIVE from the super-huge Kruger National Park in the super country of South Africa."

Steve looks out through the windows. "This is the biggest game reserve in all of Africa. Over 7500 square miles of wide-open spaces—roughly the size of Belgium. The park is home to 336 species of trees, 49 species of fish, 34 species of amphibians, 114 reptile species, 507 bird species and 147 mammal species.[1] If you're looking for animals, this is the place!"

Driving down the dirt path, they see a black rhinoceros, Cape buffaloes, African elephants, plus several leopards and lions.

"This is what they call 'The Big Five' animal group," Steve explains. "It consists of lion, African elephant, Cape buffalo, leopard and rhinoceros. It's not called The Big Five because of how big the animals are, but because of the difficulty in hunting them and the danger in being around them. That's why everyone in this park has to stay in their cars at all times. So, don't go away! We'll be right back after this."

1   "Kruger National Park," *South African National Parks,* http://www.sanparks.org/parks/kruger/ (7/10/2013).

In the other van, cameraman Harrison Borg turns off the camera by remote. They take a short break as the vans roll on through the expansive park.

"I certainly don't see any lambs out here today," Steve laughingly comments.

"If there are any lambs, they're probably hiding way up in the tallest tree," Kathleen quips.

Steve offers his ideas. "Or they're checked in at the local lamb-post hotel, or behind a heavily locked door in a castle near the land of 'Lambelot.' Or, maybe they went back into the city, riding on the 'Lamb-Tram.' Get it? Lamb-Tram?"

They can hear soundman George Lupas laughing on the intercom from the other van. But then he realizes he is the only one laughing, and coughs a few times to stop.

Kathleen turns to the driver. "OK, are there really any lambs out here, Ronnie?"

"There are different species whose young *are* called lambs: impala and antelope, among others," Ronnie adds, "but you're right, their mothers keep them secluded and as safe as possible."

"It's a dangerous place out there, living in the wild," Kathleen adds.

Harrison comes in over the walkie-talkie. "Hey boss, I've got some footage from our first week in South Africa when we visited the city of Durban. Thought I'd run it for this next segment."

Before Steve can answer, the real "boss" answers.

"That's great, Harry," Kathleen says, making notes on her UPAD. "We'll all watch it as a refresher. Start it up."

The portable monitor in both vans crackles to life, the static clears and we see Steve, reporting from a busy downtown area, about a week ago.

"South Africa, located way down at the southernmost tip of the African continent, is filled with wide open spaces where all kinds of animals roam. But it also has beautiful cities where lots of people live. It is a culturally diverse country, a nation made up of many people groups. There are 11 different official languages, and a rich variety of traditions and skin colors. African Bishop Desmond Tutu called South Africa the rainbow nation of Africa."[2]

Different scenes of South Africa flash across the screen.

"Wow, there are more than 52 million people[3] here from all different ethnic backgrounds, so you hear lots of languages, and get to try many types of food and see different ways of living. And, South Africa is big enough to be roughly three times the size of Texas and five times the size of Japan![4] And, did you know that 20 percent of the world's gold is mined here,[5] and Kimberly, South Africa, is the home of the largest diamond mine in the world?"

Suddenly, the image changes. On screen, Steve begins to look around as he hears police sirens wail in the background. People run by behind him, and he hears breaking glass.

2   "The Rainbow Nation," *SouthAfrica.info,* http://www.southafrica.info/pls/cms/show_gallery_sa_info?p_gid=2363&p_site_id=38 (7/16/13).

3   "Midyear Population Estimates, 2013." *Stats SA,* http://www.statssa.gov.za/publications/P0302/P03022013.pdf.

4   "Fun Facts About South Africa," *South Africa Explorer,* http://www.southafricaexplorer.co.za/articles/facts-about-south-africa.html, (7/16/13).

5   "Fun Facts About South Africa."

"Ladies and gentlemen, I've heard that it can get pretty rough here in the city, and I'm seeing it firsthand."

A police car whizzes by, followed by an ambulance. Then the sirens fade away.

"Historically, there have been many challenges to overcome in South Africa, but there are strong groups of believers here. They know God is with them."

The scene cuts to Steve in front of a church, talking to the pastor, a bald man in a colorful coat.

"Are you really Steve Storyberg?" the pastor asks, not sure.

"Yes sir, I am. So, Pastor John, you're seeing lots of new families fill up the seats in your church?"

"I watch your show all the time, Steve. But anyway, yes, we're so thankful, God is bringing new families to us. Even this past Sunday, we broke the record for Sunday morning attendance, and had a delicious meal after church to celebrate!"

"This is such a wonderful country, Pastor, but we know there have been difficult times." Steve looks intently at Pastor John. "How can we be praying for you?"

"Well, Steve, we need God to restore peace and hope to South Africa. He's a big God, and we know He can do it. And, we'll be here to serve Him, gentle as lambs, but strong as roaring lions!"

Suddenly, Steve hits the pause button on the remote, and the screen image freezes. He sets the remote down on the dashboard. But Kathleen, Ronnie and Steve are left thoughtfully staring at the screen.

"Those are powerful words," Steve says slowly.

"More powerful than you think!" Ronnie adds. "Don't move, look away from the screen slowly. We're not alone."

As they look through the windows, the trio is amazed to see that both vans are surrounded by large lions with golden eyes and thick, furry manes. Their white whiskers catch the sunlight, and their tails swish gently behind them.

"Steve," Kathleen says, her voice a little shaky, "I hate to tell you this right now."

"What?" asks Steve. "You're going to make a run for it?"

"No!" Kathleen whispers. "You're going LIVE in three, two, one."

"Oh, uh…This is Steve Storyberg, Superkid Academy Worldwide News, here at the Kruger National Park in South Africa. As you can see for yourself, we're safe in the van, but we're surrounded by some pretty big cats. OK. African lions. They are called *ingonyama* in Zulu, which means 'big cat.' And, those are some pretty big cats!"

Just then, a cute lion cub clambers onto the hood of the van. It looks through the windshield at Steve, and begins licking the glass.

"Well, I guess this little guy is going to grow up to be a window washer! Seriously, folks, God has not given us a spirit of fear, so right now, I am trusting in God's protection!"

The cub begins to slide off the hood and Steve holds his breath. He sees the cub on the ground, wandering away, and breathes a sigh of relief.

One by one, the lions turn and leave, moving off into the trees. The last lion disappears into the trees, leaving the vans, once again, alone on the dirt path.

Steve, Kathleen, Ronnie, George and Harrison all let out a deep sigh of relief at the same time.

Ronnie puts the engine in gear, and they slowly move forward.

Steve breaks the silence. "Well, we learned a lesson here, ladies and gentlemen. Even when you're surrounded by dangerous things, trust in God. Be gentle as lambs, and strong as roaring lions!"

In the distance, a lion, far away, roars loudly enough, it seems, to shake all of South Africa.

"Well, maybe I'll be a lion *without* the roar—don't want to scare people!"

Discussion Questions:

1. **What do you think Pastor John meant when he said Christians should be like both lambs and lions?**
2. **How do you think Joshua 1:9 ties in to this story?**
3. **Name "The Big Five" animals. Which one is your favorite and why?**
4. **How can we be praying for Christians in South Africa?**
5. **How can we be praying for the cities of South Africa?**

Variation No. 1: Additional Study

Learn more about South Africa's history, economy, natural resources and spiritual growth by checking out books at your local library. You may even find outreaches in South Africa that your family would like to support in honor of what you've learned.

Variation No. 2: KCM Africa

Visit KCM Africa's website to learn what God is doing in that country through Kenneth Copeland Ministries. Read about its history and outreach to the country of South Africa and the continent of Africa.

(For more information about Kenneth Copeland Ministries South Africa, go to kcm.org/sa.)

Variation No. 3: Map Skills

Print a blank map of South Africa from the Internet. Have your children mark the capital (Pretoria), other large cities, bordering countries and major bodies of water. Ask them to trace this map several times throughout the week to help them remember and gain better understanding of South Africa.

Notes:_____

_____

_____

DAY 3: GIVING LESSON THE PRICE IS RIGHT

Suggested Time: 10 minutes

Offering Scripture: Then those "sheep" are going to say, "Master, what are you talking about? When did we ever see you hungry and feed you, thirsty and give you a drink?" Then the King will say, "I'm telling the solemn truth: Whenever you did one of these things to someone overlooked or ignored, that was me—you did it to me." –Matthew 25:37, 40 MSG

Supplies: ☐ A small amount of money (about $8 in coins and bills), ☐ 1 Loaf of sliced bread ☐ 1 Jar of peanut butter, ☐ 1 Squeeze bottle of jelly, ☐ 3 Card-stock price cards, ☐ 3 Envelopes

(Corresponds with Lesson Outline No. I)

Prior to Lesson:

Using the card stock, prepare a price card for each of the following items: one loaf of bread, one jar of peanut butter and one squeeze bottle of jelly.

Write the purchase amount on each card. Place each item on a table, with the price card in front of it, but with the blank side facing the children, so the price cannot be seen. Place the cash amount of each item into three corresponding envelopes.

Allow the children to open one envelope at a time, count the money and guess which of the three items could be purchased with the money.

Lesson Instructions:

Isn't it fun to go grocery shopping? On this table are three items: one jar of peanut butter, one loaf of bread and one squeeze bottle of jelly. Let's open the envelopes one at a time, count the money and work together to guess which item the money in the envelope can buy.

Let's see if you guessed correctly. *(Take a moment and reveal the actual price of each item.)*

Great job! This activity can help us realize that even a small amount of money and time can show God's love toward others, and it honors God. We were able to purchase a whole jar of peanut butter, a loaf of bread and a squeeze bottle of jelly for a small amount of money. God is not looking for the biggest offering. He is looking at the heart attitude of the giver.

We don't have to be an adult or have a "grown-up" job to honor God and bless other people. It's the little ways we choose to share God's goodness and love with others that produce fruit and blessings in our lives and in the lives of those we are helping.

If we work together and take food to a homeless shelter, it would be just like fixing a yummy peanut butter and jelly sandwich for Jesus!

Notes:_____

_____

_____

_____

_____

_____

_____

_____

_____

_____

_____

_____

_____

_____

_____

_____

_____

_____

_____

_____

_____

_____

_____

_____

_____

_____

_____

_____

_____

_____

_____

_____

_____

_____

_____

_____

DAY 4: OBJECT LESSON — **MASTER SEED**

 Suggested Time: 10 minutes

 Key Scripture: For God's love has been poured out in our hearts through the Holy Spirit Who has been given to us. –Romans 5:5 AMP

Supplies: ■ 5 Different fruit samples (ex: apple, orange, strawberry, cherry, kiwi or watermelon), ■ 1 Container

(Corresponds with Lesson Outline No. I, II)

Prior to Lesson:

Choose five different fruits that contain a seed. Remove the seed from each fruit and place the seeds in a container to share with the kids. Display a sample of each whole piece of fruit and a sample of each fruit with the seed removed.

Lesson Instructions:

Today, we'll be discussing fruit. We have several different pieces of fruit here. Can anyone tell me what all this fruit has in common? *(Allow time for your children to share and discuss their ideas.)*

Yes! All the fruit items have seeds! Earlier, I removed the seeds from each piece of fruit, and placed them in a container. *(Allow time for your children to view the seeds and guess which fruit each seed came from.)*

Over the next couple of months, we'll be learning about fruit, but it's not the kind of fruit we eat. The fruit we'll be discussing is the kind of fruit the Bible calls "the fruit of the spirit." Now, don't go looking for a "spirit fruit" tree because this kind of fruit doesn't grow on trees. This kind of fruit grows in your heart—your spirit. Something else that's cool about the fruit of the spirit is there are different kinds of spirit fruit, just like there are all kinds of regular fruit.

But, remember how all the seeds from the fruit shown in this lesson are different? Well, spirit fruit doesn't have different kinds of seeds! You may be thinking, *Wait a minute, how can that be?* No, there is just one kind of seed that grows spirit fruit. Let's read our Object Lesson scripture together from Romans 5:5 AMP. It says, "God's love has been poured out in our hearts through the Holy Spirit Who has been given to us." How awesome is that? God plants one seed in our hearts that grows all kinds of wonderful things. It's the seed of His love. But don't be concerned, we won't have apples sprouting out of our ears! But with the seed of God's love planted in our hearts, we can have all kinds of great spirit fruit growing out of us in no time!

Variation: Garden Study

Consider visiting your local library for children's books on gardening and how seeds work. There are several parallels between physical seeds and spiritual seeds, such as: Scientists believe one reason fruit is sweet is because the sweetness entices birds and animals to eat the fruit and spread the seeds. In the same way, God uses sweet fruit of the spirit in us to spread His love.

When you plant a seed, you must wait patiently for it to grow. Successful gardening takes effort and patience. In order to harvest a specific fruit, you must plant a specific seed. In other words, you can't plant an apple seed and expect oranges, just as you can't plant anger and expect to harvest love.

Notes:_____

_____

_____

_____

_____

_____

_____

_____

_____

_____

_____

_____

_____

_____

_____

_____

_____

_____

_____

_____

_____

_____

_____

DAY 5: GAME TIME **TOWER STACK**

 Suggested Time: 10 minutes

 Memory Verse: I have revealed you to them, and I will continue to do so. Then your love for me will be in them, and I will be in them. —John 17:26

 Teacher Tip: Stacking boxes (or "nesting" boxes) can be found at craft stores in multiple sizes.

Supplies: ◼ Set of stacking boxes, ◼ A timer (or stopwatch) ◼ Prize for the winner

(Corresponds with Lesson Outline No. III)

Prior to Game:

Prepare a safe route for your children to walk while carrying the stacked boxes. You may complete this task inside or outdoors. Place the unstacked (or "unnested") boxes on 1 side of a room or yard.

Game Instructions:

Today, we'll challenge each other in a box-stacking, course-walking contest! You will stack the boxes (largest on the bottom to smallest on the top) and carry the stacked boxes, while walking the course. If a box is dropped while you are walking the course, you will have to stop, pick up the box, place it back on the tower and then proceed to the finish.

Game Goal:

The player with the fastest course time, wins the prize!

Final Word:

Walking with an unsteady tower of boxes can be challenging, just as walking through life without the spirit of love is unsteady and challenging, too. But, when we walk with the spirit of love, we never fail!

Notes:_____

_____

_____

_____

_____

ACTIVITY PAGE   **PETER AND THE BEGGAR CROSSWORD**

 Memory Verse: I have revealed you to them, and I will continue to do so. Then your love for me will be in them, and I will be in them. –John 17:26

(Corresponds with Lesson Outline No. I)

This week you learned about showing God's love to others, just as Peter did with the beggar at the Beautiful Gate. Using words from this week's Bible lesson (Acts 3:1-11), complete this crossword puzzle.

Across

3. Lovely to the senses

5. An opening for entering or leaving a yard or walled area

6. To make or grow strong or stronger

9. A series of columns that holds up a roof or beam

Down

1. A building or place for religious worship

2. Made whole or healthy again

4. Without delay; immediately

6. A shiny white metal that lots of jewelry is made from

7. The coins or paper notes of a country used to buy things or pay for services

8. Not able to walk well

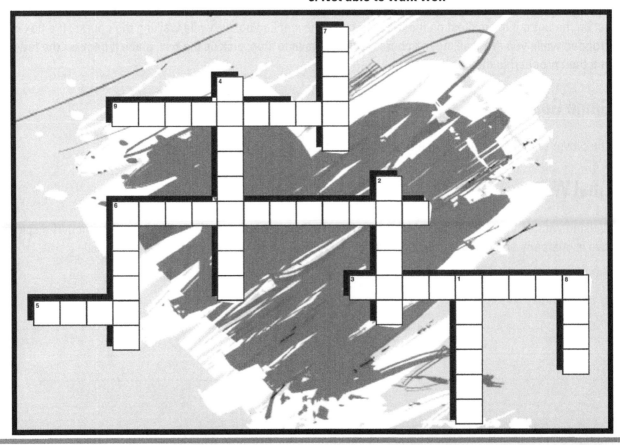

ANSWER KEY:

Notes:

_____

_____

_____

_____

_____

_____

_____

_____

_____

_____

_____

_____

WEEK 3: LOVE UNSTOPPABLE

 Memory Verse: Love never fails [never fades out or becomes obsolete or comes to an end].
—1 Corinthians 13:8a AMP

45

WEEK 3: SNAPSHOT — LOVE UNSTOPPABLE

DAY	TYPE OF LESSON	LESSON TITLE	SUPPLIES
Day 1	Bible Lesson	Jesus and Love	None
Day 2	Real Deal	Gladys Aylward	Picture of Gladys Aylward, Costume (optional)
Day 3	Giving Lesson	Keep Faith Flowing	1 Punch ball or 1 large balloon
Day 4	Storybook Theater	Bubble Gum and Dogs	Whiteboard or chalkboard or easel with paper, Dry-erase markers if using whiteboard, Colored chalks if using a chalkboard, Pencil (art pencils work best) and eraser and black marker and rags (to blend chalks) if using paper, Art smock
Day 5	Game Time	Jump 'n Jingle Relay	2 Jingle bells, 2 Beach balls, 2 Rubber cones, Upbeat music (optional)
Bonus	Activity Page	How Many Words?	1 Copy for each child

Lesson Instruction:

We've doubled up on our teaching about love in this volume of the *Superkid Academy Home Bible Study* because all the other "fruit" fall into place behind love. Faith, patience, joy and all the others, come out of love. Anything we try to do on our own without using God's powerful nature inside us is done in our flesh.

During this study of the fruit of the spirit, refer often to the difference between walking in the flesh and walking in the spirit. What we do in the flesh is just hard work, but what we do in the spirit is empowered by Him!

An important concept for the kids to take away from this series is that for every pressure, or lust of the flesh, Satan brings, there is a force that comes out of you when you choose love, joy, peace, patience, gentleness, goodness, faithfulness, kindness and self-control. Satan has *nothing* that can defeat us when we walk in the spirit. Our Superkids are winners in God!

Love,

Commander Kellie

Commander Kellie

Lesson Outline:

This week, you will be teaching your children that God's love never ends. This is important for them to understand because God's love is complete. It covers their past, present and future. As they follow God and obey His commandments, they will begin to live lives of love.

Throughout the coming week, begin sharing the points below with your children. Take this teaching beyond the scripted lessons by working them into your conversations. Help your children meditate on the following phrases: "love never fails," "walking in love" and "producing everlasting fruit." These can be abstract concepts, but help your children understand and think of ways to apply them.

I. GOD'S WORD SAYS "LOVE NEVER FAILS" 1 Corinthians 13:8 AMP

a. Our natural love can fail.

b. When love is first place, we don't fall for Satan's tricks.

c. The devil CAN'T HANDLE GOD'S LOVE!!!

d. Love confuses the enemy.

II. JESUS COMMANDED THAT WE WALK IN LOVE John 15:12

a. He chose to love even when men came to arrest Him.

b. Natural weapons do not have the power that love has.

c. Jesus defeated death because He walked in God's love.

III. WALKING IN LOVE PRODUCES EVERLASTING FRUIT! John 15:16-17

a. Satan continually attempts to pressure you into not loving others.

b. He will try to get you into strife with people. He even tries to get strong Superkids like you to fight with their brothers or sisters!

c. There is no law against the fruit of love. Nothing can defeat God in you when you choose to let His nature come out! Galatians 5:22-23

d. If we walk in love, we can have whatever we ask. Galatians 5:6 says our faith works by love.

e. Satan doesn't want us to know these secrets to success. Too bad and too late—God already has a bunch of Superkids who know the truth about the fruit of love!

Notes:_____

_____

_____

DAY 1: BIBLE LESSON
JESUS AND LOVE

Memory Verse: Love never fails [never fades out or becomes obsolete or comes to an end].
−1 Corinthians 13:8a AMP

(Corresponds with Lesson Outline No. II-III)

There's no better place to learn about God's idea of love than from His Son, Jesus. Today, your children will learn how to show love to God and others.

Read John 15:9-17:
Jesus Speaks to the Disciples About Love

"I have loved you even as the Father has loved me. Remain in my love. When you obey my commandments, you remain in my love, just as I obey my Father's commandments and remain in his love. I have told you these things so that you will be filled with my joy. Yes, your joy will overflow! This is my commandment: Love each other in the same way I have loved you. There is no greater love than to lay down one's life for one's friends. You are my friends if you do what I command. I no longer call you slaves, because a master doesn't confide in his slaves. Now you are my friends, since I have told you everything the Father told me. You didn't choose me. I chose you. I appointed you to go and produce lasting fruit, so that the Father will give you whatever you ask for, using my name. This is my command: Love each other."

Discussion Questions:

1. **What was Jesus' message to His disciples?**

   Jesus shared how important it was to love other people as He has loved us.

2. **How can we show Jesus that we love Him?**

   We show Jesus we love Him when we obey the Father's commandments.

3. **Why do you think obedience and love are so closely connected?**

   Obedience is an action that communicates an attitude. If you love God, you want to live in a way that pleases Him and reflects His nature, which is love.

4. **What does Jesus mean when He says, "There is no greater love than to lay down one's life for one's friends"?**

   Jesus is telling us to put others and their needs before our own.

5. **What does Jesus mean when He says to "produce lasting fruit"?**

   The fruit of love is lasting fruit because God is love, and His love never fails. When we walk in His love by putting others ahead of ourselves and loving them, we are walking in Him and manifesting what He is like to others.

6. **How can you produce the fruit of love?**

Answers will vary. Encourage your children to identify specific ways they can live a life of love. Examples could include obeying their parents, completing their chores without complaining, and sharing with and caring for their siblings.

Notes:

DAY 2: REAL DEAL

GLADYS AYLWARD

 Memory Verse: Love never fails [never fades out or becomes obsolete or comes to an end].
−1 Corinthians 13:8a AMP

 Concept: Highlighting an interesting historical place, figure or event that illustrates the theme of the day. The theme of the day is *God's love never fails.*

 Media: If you have the technical capability, show media photos of Gladys Aylward. If you do not have this capability, you may print out photos from the Internet to show the kids or check out a book from your local library.

Supplies: ■ Costume optional (see Variation No. 1 on page 54)

(Corresponds with Lesson Outline I, III)

Intro:

Today, you will highlight an interesting historical figure for your children—Gladys Aylward (AIL-wood). The purpose of this lesson is to use real-life people and events to illustrate the theme of the day, which is *God's love never fails.*

Jesus is the ultimate example of unfailing love. He chose to love even when He wasn't loved in return and when others chose to persecute Him. Today, we'll learn about a woman who demonstrated this never-ending, God-kind of love and dedicated her life to loving people.

Lesson Instructions:

This week we're learning about God's unfailing love.

Can someone remind me of this week's Bible memory verse? *(Allow for answers.)*

About Gladys Aylward:

Gladys Aylward was born in Edmonton, East London, England, in 1902. Born into a working-class family, Gladys had little formal education and at age 14 became a parlormaid for a wealthy family. But, at the age of 18, Gladys' life changed forever. She went to hear an evangelist preach about Jesus and chose to dedicate her life to serving God and others. After reading a magazine article about faraway China and the millions of people who hadn't heard about Jesus, she knew in her heart she wanted to be a missionary to China.

Unstoppable Determination:

Challenge No. 1: Little Education: Gladys faced many obstacles as she stepped toward the calling God placed on her heart. When Gladys was in her mid-20s, she entered a missionary school in London, called the China

Inland Mission Center. Gladys was unable to complete the exams, and was kindly told she was not a suitable missionary candidate. The school officials felt she would not be capable of learning the complex Chinese language. They also wanted someone who was younger and more able to adapt.[1] Gladys was very disappointed, but continued to persevere in her calling, despite this apparent setback.

Challenge No. 2: Money and a Dangerous Trip: While working as a maid in the home of Sir Francis Younghusband who had been a famous British military officer and explorer in India, Tibet and the Far East, Gladys was able to borrow books from his extensive library. It was there she learned of an elderly Scottish missionary living in China named Jeannie Lawson, who had written, asking for someone to come and help her. Gladys saw this as her opportunity and wrote to the elderly missionary accepting the request. Mrs. Lawson could not help with Gladys' transportation to China, so Gladys worked nights and weekends to save money for her trip. She wasn't able to save enough money for ship fare, so Gladys chose to take the Trans-Siberian Railway. This was a very dangerous way to travel in those days, especially for a single woman. But with her determination and God's grace, after a few very close calls in the middle of war zones, she arrived safely in Yangchuan, China.

Loving the Chinese People:

Being a foreigner and a woman in China was challenging. The Chinese people did not trust her or any foreigner, nor want to learn from her. Gladys had another opportunity to be discouraged and allow her natural love to fail, but she allowed God's love to prevail in her, instead.

Jeannie and Gladys decided to work together to convert their rented residence into an inn, providing clean lodging, good food and Bible stories to mule-team drivers and travelers. She learned a lot from serving with Jeannie, and Gladys' consistent presence began to earn the trust of many Chinese people. She studied the Chinese language every day and became fluent in it.

One day, after Gladys had gone out, Mrs. Lawson, now an elderly woman, sustained a severe fall. Though Gladys tried to nurse her back to health, after 50 years of missionary work in China, Jeannie Lawson went home to be with the Lord a few days later. Gladys was now left alone at the inn with only one Chinese servant—a Christian convert—to help her. Gladys remained in China, becoming a Chinese citizen in 1936[2] and continuing to let her light shine by showing love to the people of China.

One day, there was a riot in the local prison. The top magistrate, the "Mandarin," asked that Gladys go into the middle of it and stop the riot. There were already several men dead on the ground and a tall man with a knife had blood all over him. Gladys stood shaking at the entrance. "Why me?" she gasped. The warden challenged, "You tell us your God is all-powerful. Is He, or is He not?"

"He is," she declared, seeking to bolster her courage, as she stepped into the sandy courtyard. "But, only through the help of Jesus will I prevail, for the gospel of God in our Bible states, 'I can do all things through Him who strengthens me.'"[3]

Gladys prayed, and the Lord helped this little, 4-foot, 10-inch woman to walk boldly into the midst of the mayhem and shout for quiet. She demanded the knife be given to her, that the men form into ranks and a

---

1   "Small Woman, Big Heart, Great Faith," by Jack Voelkel, Urbana for God's Global Mission, Intervarsity, https://urbana.org/go-and-do/missionary-biographies/small-woman-big-heart-great-faith (5/15/13).

2   "Gladys Aylward's 'Impossible Mission' to China," Christianity.com, http://www.christianity.com/church/church-history/timeline/1901-2000/gladys-aylwards-impossible-mission-to-china-11630754.html (5/15/13).

3   "Small Woman, Big Heart, Great Faith."

spokesman come forward to tell her of the prisoners' grievances. She found out that the prison conditions were miserable and the prisoners had very little food aside from what relatives could bring. Gladys had some ideas. She insisted the men should be given looms so they could weave cloth to make better clothing for themselves and to sell some as well. She also asked for a mill so the men could grind grain—all of which she received. Gladys visited the men often to tell them about Jesus. One of the leaders of the prisoners, Feng, accepted Jesus as his Savior[4] and later became a great help to her.

This incident gained Gladys great respect from the Chinese people. She became known as *Ai-weh-deh,* which means "Virtuous One."

Love Unstoppable:

In China, many children without parents were bought and sold as slaves. Gladys knew these children needed God's love and care, so she began rescuing them. The inn soon became a shelter and an orphanage.

During those years, with the invasion of Japan, war broke out in China, threatening Gladys and her work with the orphans. She also began taking in and nursing many wounded Chinese soldiers. But, soon, Gladys would face one of her biggest challenges. The Japanese Army was getting closer to their village and the bombings were becoming more frequent. Gladys was urged to leave the area. She eventually fled on foot over the rugged mountains with 100 orphaned children—some of them infants. Gladys was alone in her mission but trusted in Jesus to guide her way across 100 miles of mountainous terrain.

After 12 days of the 27-day journey over the mountains, an obstacle appeared—the Yellow River, with no easy way to cross. The children knelt down and began praying. They knew God could help them. Not long after they prayed and sang songs, some Nationalist soldiers who had heard the singing, helped them get across the river to safety.

While Gladys was alone one day, some Japanese soldiers saw her and started shooting at her. Gladys ran into a field of grain with bullets zinging around her, ripping through her clothes and one grazing her back.[5] The Lord helped her escape, and she was able to continue the long journey and bring all 100 children safely to Xian. After Gladys delivered the children into caring, competent hands, she collapsed into a semi-coma for several days, sick with typhus, pneumonia, recurring fevers, malnutrition and extreme exhaustion.[6] After she recovered, Gladys went back to ministry, sharing the gospel in the local villages with lepers and in prisons.

Making History:

Gladys Aylward answered the call on her life to love others, travel to a foreign country and share God's goodness with people who did not initially welcome her. Gladys walked in love with the Chinese people and eventually won their hearts. Her strength and faith were stretched, but God's love in her did not fail.

Outro:

Giving, being kind and laying down one's life to help others comes from a heart full of God's love. Gladys Aylward lived a life of never-ending love and brought peace and hope to many Chinese people.

---

4   "Small Woman, Big Heart, Great Faith."
5   "Small Woman, Big Heart, Great Faith."
6   "Gladys Aylward's 'Impossible Mission' to China."

That's what makes Gladys and her story today's Real Deal.

Variation No. 1: Dress Up

Bring Gladys Aylward's life front and center by dressing up in period costumes. Use the everyday things you have around your home and have fun with it! Instruct your children to dress in what they think a person in 19th century England would wear. For girls, think floor-length dresses in muted colors (ex: "prairie" or "English collar"). For boys, think dark jackets, top hats and vests. You could even have a contest to see who comes up with the most original or most accurate costume. Perhaps the winner could be rewarded with a homemade dinner of his/her choice!

Variation No. 2: Teen Helper

Let your teen present this lesson to his/her younger siblings. In addition to the above points, he/she could research more about Gladys Aylward and bring what is learned to life in a creative way.

Variation No. 3: Biography

Read a biography of Gladys Aylward to your children. You could read one chapter each night to your children before bed, and discuss it. Let today's lesson be an introduction to an even deeper study of this brave and selfless woman.

Variation No. 4: Map Skills

Have your children locate on a map or globe the places discussed in this lesson: China and the city of Yangchuan.

Notes:_____

_____

_____

_____

_____

_____

_____

_____

_____

_____

_____

_____

DAY 3: GIVING LESSON

KEEP FAITH FLOWING

Suggested Time: *10 minutes*

Offering Scripture: *...faith working through love.* –Galatians 5:6 NKJV

Supplies: ■ *1 Punch ball or 1 large balloon*

(Corresponds with Lesson Outline No. III)

Prior to Lesson:

Leave a deflated punch ball or balloon in the middle of your living room floor or in the middle of your kitchen table. The punch ball or balloon will be inflated as the lesson is taught. *(Consider also having an inflated punch ball or balloon available prior to the lesson.)*

Lesson Instructions:

Does anyone like to play with punch balls or balloons? Balloons and punch balls are fun, but this one seems to have a challenge. Does anyone know what it needs? You're right! It needs air!

Would anyone like to help with the demonstration by adding air to this balloon or punch ball? *(Choose a volunteer to help with the demonstration.)* Thank you for volunteering! As you continue to blow air into the balloon, it continues to get bigger and bigger.

Let's think of the air that fills this balloon (or punch ball) as our faith. As we learn to believe and trust in God's promises, our faith grows bigger and bigger, just like this punch ball. *(Allow the balloon to get bigger, but do not tie off the bottom.)*

Let's say our offering scripture together from Galatians 5:6 NKJV: "...faith working through love." Receiving God's love into our hearts and then allowing that love to flow out of us into the lives of others will help our love to grow. With God's love working in us, we'll want to be kind, respectful and generous to others. When God's love is not working in us, it's like this balloon leaking air—it gets smaller and smaller. *(Allow some air to leak out of the balloon or punch ball.)*

There are behaviors that can keep our faith from working: If we are greedy or disrespectful, or if we are not kind to our brothers and sisters, then love is not working in our lives. This is what happens to our "faith balloon." *(Allow some air to leak out of the balloon.)* So, let's try this again. *(Blow air back into the balloon.)* Now, our balloon is full of "faith air," and this time we'll make sure we keep our attitude right and do things that please God. When we do, it's like taking our balloon and tying a knot in the end. We could call it the "love knot."

Remember, kids, keep the "air of faith" in your giving and make sure to watch over your heart. With the "love knot" in place, our faith stays right where it needs to be!

Now, let's get our offering ready to take to church this week.

Notes:_____

_____

_____

_____

_____

_____

_____

_____

_____

_____

_____

_____

_____

_____

_____

_____

_____

_____

_____

_____

_____

_____

_____

_____

_____

_____

_____

DAY 4: STORYBOOK THEATER

BUBBLE GUM AND DOGS

Teacher Tip: This segment has many possible variations. Choose the one that best fits your family, and have fun!

List of Characters/Costumes:

- Donald: Messy hair and an old T-shirt
- Mr. Goodman: Suit jacket, white shirt and nice tie
- Mrs. Goodman: Dress, pearls and a straw hat
- Miss Berry: Glasses and her hair in a bun
- Mr. Stark: Comb-over hair and mustache (mustache can be drawn with an eyeliner pencil)
- Rosie: Pigtails and freckles (freckles can be drawn with a brown eyeliner pencil)

Supplies: ■ Whiteboard or chalkboard or easel with paper, ■ Dry-erase markers if using whiteboard, ■ Colored chalks if using a chalkboard, ■ Pencil (art pencils work best) and eraser and colored chalk and black marker and rags (to blend chalks) if using paper, ■ Art smock (to keep your artist's clothes clean)

(Corresponds with Lesson Outline No. I, III d)

Variation No. 1: Read the story as part of your read-aloud time.

Variation No. 2:

Read the story as an old-time radio skit, complete with different actors for each part. If you are limited on participants, then have each person play more than one part and change the voice for each character. Make copies of the skit and have each actor highlight their lines.

Variation No. 3:

Act out the story as a fun skit. Perhaps your children can practice during the day (even creating fun costumes from everyday items) and then perform it in the evening for the whole family. Before beginning your skit, remember to introduce your cast!

Variation No. 4:

Create a storybook theater where one or more family members sketch the story on a whiteboard, chalkboard or artist's easel as another member reads the story. Initially, there will be a few supplies to purchase but don't let this be a deterrent from using the illustrated story option! Once the supplies have been purchased, they'll be long-lasting and reusable.

To make your presentation easier, lightly sketch the drawing with a pencil prior to presentation. Time may not allow the picture to be completely drawn and colored at the time of the lesson. Erase the pencil lines, so light lines are visible to the artist, but are not obvious to your children. Review the story ahead of time to determine the amount of time needed to complete the illustration while telling the story. When the story begins, use black markers to "draw" the picture, following the sketched pencil lines. Next, apply color using the pastel chalk. Then, blend the color with the rags. Finally, cut the illustration from the board, roll it up, secure it with rubber bands and share it with one of your children!

Story:

Through the gate, down the walk and behind the two big, brown doors of Weeping Willow Children's Home, is a variety of kids—big kids, little kids, loud kids, quiet kids and kids of all colors. Even though each child is very different, they all have one thing in common: they're all orphans. Each is waiting to be loved. This story is about one of those very special orphans.

Donald has dark brown hair, and when he smiles, it causes his eyes to squint. And Donald smiles a lot! Today is Donald's seventh birthday and every year he asks for the same presents: bubble gum and a dog. Every year Donald is told, "No pets allowed at Weeping Willow. No gum allowed either; it sticks to the floors."

"But, I promise I won't drop my gum on the floor! I just want to know what it tastes like," Donald pleads.

"No gum."

This birthday is very special because Donald received the best birthday news ever! Miss Berry, a worker at the orphanage, has told him there is a foster family ready to take him home.

"What's a foster family? Does that mean their last name is `Foster'?" Donald asked.

"No, a foster family is a family who's willing to take care of you for a while," Miss Berry replied.

"How long is a while?" Donald wondered.

"That's decided by the foster family. It could be for one month or longer," Miss Berry replied.

"I'm going to be extra good, so they'll want to keep me forever! And I'll show them my coolest magic trick!" he exclaimed.

"Don't get too excited. Not many kids get adopted because most people want to adopt a baby."

Donald's heart sank and his ever-present smile drooped. Miss Berry's words played over and over again in his head: "Most people want a baby." If only he had a dog right now; a dog would love him whether he was 2 or 92. Oh well, at least he would be out of the orphanage for a while and experience many new things. He was just starting to daydream when Miss Berry snapped him out of it.

Donald needed to get his things together because the foster family would be picking him up in one hour. Donald headed up the rickety staircase to the room he shared with 11 other boys.

Creeeeeak, crack. Creeeeeak, crack. The stairs made funny noises. Donald pulled a cardboard box from under the small, metal-frame bed. This box contained everything he owned, so it didn't take long to pack. He stuffed a few extra belongings—a ragged bear, a toothbrush and a bouncing ball—into his pillowcase and headed down the stairs.

Creeeeeak, crack. Creeeeeak, crack.

"Whew! I won't miss these creaky stairs," Donald said to himself.

A little, freckle-faced girl named Rosie came skipping up to Donald. "What are you doing?" she asked.

"Waiting for my foster family," Donald replied.

"Why would anyone pick you? You don't even have all your teeth," she added, then skipped off before he had time to answer her.

Why would anyone pick him? Maybe Miss Berry and the freckle-faced girl were right. Maybe he wasn't special enough to be loved. He sat down on the hard, wooden bench by the door to wait. A big, white clock on the wall looked back at him. *Tick tock, tick tock.* He watched the little hands on the clock move. Thirty minutes went by, then another hour. Donald rested his chin on his hands. Maybe this wasn't such a great birthday after all.

Rosie popped her head around the corner. "Still not here?" she asked.

He thought about throwing his pillowcase at Rosie but she'd definitely tattle and get him in trouble. Not worth it. Instead, he just looked out the window.

Three more hours passed, and a loud bell sounded. Dinnertime. Donald wasn't very hungry. The disappointment had stolen his appetite. He felt a tap on his shoulder and swung around. But it was just Miss Berry.

"Dinnertime, Donald," she said.

"I have to wait for my foster family."

"I'm sorry, son. I don't think they're coming or they'd have been here by now," she said, while putting her hand on his shoulder.

"Come now, we're having your favorite meal: coleslaw and fried chicken!" she exclaimed.

Donald grabbed his pillowcase and headed for dinner. He got in line, took a tray, and sat down to eat with 50 other kids who probably didn't really like coleslaw. After dinner, he threw his trash away and sat down to hear the cafeteria cleaning assignments, just like he'd done a thousand times before.

Just then a pleasant-looking couple walked into the dining hall with the home director, Mr. Stark. The lady wore a nice-looking, yellow dress and heels, while the man had the coolest umbrella with a wooden duck on the handle.

Mr. Stark motioned toward Donald. An older boy sitting next to Donald jabbed him in the ribs, "Get over there, Mr. Stark is calling you."

Donald's heart pounded like a big, bass drum. He grabbed his pillowcase and wondered if this could be his foster family. He slowly walked toward the couple.

"Mr. and Mrs. Goodman, this is Donald. Donald, I'd like you to meet your foster family. Do you have your things together, son?" Mr. Stark asked.

Donald lifted up his pillowcase and felt a smile creep back to his face. He quickly told this smile to go away; it was too soon to be happy. After all, people only wanted to keep babies, not boys, and he was even missing some teeth.

Mrs. Goodman gently reached for Donald's hand and led him to their shiny, red car, which had that new-leather smell. "I heard that today is your birthday," said Mrs. Goodman.

"Yep, 7," Donald answered, holding up seven fingers.

"Well, then, this calls for a celebration! Mr. Goodman, this boy needs some birthday cake and presents!" she exclaimed.

"Yes, ma'am. Cake and presents coming right up," he said.

Donald could hardly believe it. He pinched his arm to see if this was a dream. Ouch! Nope, it was real all right. How could they be so nice? They just met him.

Mr. Goodman pulled into the parking lot of a fancy bakery. Inside, Donald ate the most amazing birthday cake. Chocolate fudge with tons of delicious icing and seven birthday candles! He'd always wanted to blow out birthday candles.

"Make a wish," Mrs. Goodman said.

It didn't take Donald long, he knew exactly what he wanted to wish for: bubble gum and a dog. He took a deep breath and blew with all his might, and the candles flickered out. Now that was fun!

"What did you wish for?" Mr. Goodman asked.

"You don't have to tell us if you don't want to share, Donald," Mrs. Goodman added.

"Ummm, it's OK. I wished for some bubble gum. I've heard it's really good."

"Anything else?" Mr. Goodman pried.

"A dog; I've always wanted a dog," Donald answered.

"Hmmmmm. Bubble gum and dogs," Mr. Goodman thought, and scratched his head. "We'd better get going, Mrs. Goodman, we've got important things to do."

With that, Mrs. Goodman grabbed Donald's hand and they drove to a pet store. Donald just sat there.

"Well, what are you waiting for? Let's get you a dog," Mr. Goodman said. NOW, he must be dreaming. Another pinch. Ouch! Nope, still awake. Before they reached the door of the pet store, Donald spotted a bubble-gum machine! Happy birthday to him! "How about that?" Mr. Goodman said, pulling out a quarter.

Within 30 seconds a huge, blue gumball tumbled into Donald's hand. He put it in his mouth and chomped down. It was delicious! How could anyone outlaw gum?! Before long the teeth he still had were bright blue. *Too cool,* he thought.

Donald's eyes were huge as he entered the pet store; he'd never seen so many animals in one place. Lizards, hamsters, fish and bunnies, but the dogs were best. Most of them were sleeping, but one little, silky-eared puppy stood looking at him. He put out his hand, and the puppy licked the glass. *Now* there was no stopping Donald's famous smile. It was back in full force.

"That's him! Look, he likes me!" Donald jumped.

"He certainly does. What will you name him?" Mr. Goodman asked.

Donald paused, and thought, "Bubble Gum. I'll call him Bubble Gum."

After Mr. Goodman paid the pet-store lady, the Goodmans, Donald and Bubble Gum got into the car and went home. Bubble Gum sat on Donald's lap and licked his hand the entire way home.

By the time Donald and Bubble Gum settled in at the Goodmans' house, it was time for bed. This was the first time Donald remembered not minding bedtime. On the big, clean bed in Donald's bedroom was a pair of nice, new pajamas. He'd never worn anything so comfy in his life! He put them on and climbed into the crisp, cool sheets, pulling the fluffy comforter up to his chin.

Just then Mr. and Mrs. Goodman entered the room. They sat at the edge of Donald's bed, holding hands. "Donald, we wanted to talk to you before bed," Mr. Goodman said.

Donald's heart sank. So, this *was* all too good to be true. Oh well, at least he'd been able to have birthday candles, gum and a dog, if only for one day.

"How would you like to live with us...forever?" Mrs. Goodman asked.

"Forever? But I thought people only wanted to keep babies," Donald answered.

Mrs. Goodman smiled and looked at Mr. Goodman. "Remember how you knew Bubble Gum was the dog for you the moment you saw him? That's exactly how we felt the moment we saw you."

"God told us you were just right for us," Mr. Goodman explained.

"But how could you want me? I don't even have my front teeth," Donald asked.

Mr. Goodman replied, "Easy. We know how much Jesus loves you. And His love is the biggest and greatest love. It's unstoppable. Jesus doesn't mind if you don't have all your teeth, or whether you're a baby or a boy. That's the kind of love we have for you. So what do you say? Can we be your parents?"

Donald's throat tightened as he felt a tear run down his face. But it wasn't a sad tear. This was a best-birthday-of-your-whole-life tear. Bubble gum, a dog and now a real family, forever!

Donald smiled so hard it made his cheeks hurt. He threw his arms around Mr. and Mrs. Goodman's necks and squeezed as tight as he could.

"I think that's a yes!" Mrs. Goodman said.

"Well, it's late, and we need to get some rest. We'll see you, son, in the morning," Mr. Goodman winked. Mr. and Mrs. Goodman turned to leave the room, switching off the bedroom light.

Donald spoke up, "Can I ask just one more question?"

"Sure."

"What should I call you?" Donald asked.

"I think most kids call their parents Mom and Dad," Mr. Goodman grinned.

THE END

Story by Jennifer Drennen

Notes:_____

_____

_____

DAY 5: GAME TIME

JUMP 'N JINGLE RELAY

Suggested Time: 5-7 minutes

Memory Verse: *Love never fails [never fades out or becomes obsolete or comes to an end].*
–1 Corinthians 13:8a AMP

Supplies: ☐ 2 Jingle bells, ☐ 2 Beach balls, ☐ 2 Rubber cones, ☐ *Upbeat music to play during the game* (optional)

(Corresponds with Lesson Outline No. I, III)

Prior to Game:

Divide players into 2 relay teams. Place masking tape on the floor to create a starting line, which can also serve as the finish line. If space is an issue, play this game outdoors and mark your starting line with rubber cones or household objects placed at opposite ends of the relay area.

Game Instructions:

Contestants will hold a jingle bell in one hand and a beach ball between their knees. As the relay begins, each player will walk or hop around the cone that has been placed at the opposite end of the room, while ringing the bell and keeping the beach ball between their knees.

As each player reaches the finish line, he/she will gently tag his/her teammate, who will continue the relay.

Game Goal:

The first team to successfully complete the course, wins.

Final Word:

God's love is unconditional and never fails. When we work together as a team, supporting and encouraging each other, we are producing good fruit that brings honor to God.

Notes:_____

_____

_____

_____

_____

ACTIVITY PAGE **HOW MANY WORDS?**

 Memory Verse: *Love never fails [never fades out or becomes obsolete or comes to an end].*
−1 Corinthians 13:8a AMP

(Corresponds with Lesson Outline No. I, III)

This week, you've learned that God's love is everlasting, or unending. Today, use this sheet to find how many words (three letters or more) you can make from the letters in the word EVERLASTING. Try to find at least 30.

EVERLASTING

1 _____ 11 _____ 21 _____

2 _____ 12 _____ 22 _____

3 _____ 13 _____ 23 _____

4 _____ 14 _____ 24 _____

5 _____ 15 _____ 25 _____

6 _____ 16 _____ 26 _____

7 _____ 17 _____ 27 _____

8 _____ 18 _____ 28 _____

9 _____ 19 _____ 29 _____

10 _____ 20 _____ 30 _____

ANSWER KEY:

There are more than 1,000 words that can be made from the letters in the word EVERLASTING. Here are some of the most common:

age	enlarge	greet	rage	sang	strange
agent	enter	grin	rail	sat	tail
agree	entire	invest	rain	satin	tan
air	erase	lane	ran	save	ten
alert	eternal	last	rang	sea	tiger
alien	evangelist	late	rant	seen	tin
align	even	lean	rave	servant	trail
alive	event	learn	real	serve	train
angel	evil	lease	reign	seven	travel
antler	gain	least	relate	sign	tree
ant	gait	leave	relative	signal	trial
are	gas	leg	relevant	sing	triangle
art	gave	let	rental	single	vain
ate	gear	lever	rest	siren	van
avenge	gentle	line	retail	slang	vase
eager	giant	listen	retain	slant	vast
earnest	girl	liter	reveal	slave	vein
earn	give	liver	ring	snag	versatile
ease	grain	native	rinse	snail	verse
easier	grant	near	risen	snare	veteran
east	grave	neat	rival	stain	vinegar
eastern	gravesite	negative	sail	stair	vine
eat	grease	nerve	saint	starve	
elegant	great	nest	sale	steel	
else	green	never	salt	sterile	

WEEK 4: JOY

Memory Verse: *Don't be dejected and sad, for the joy of the Lord is your strength!* —Nehemiah 8:10b

WEEK 4: SNAPSHOT

JOY

DAY	TYPE OF LESSON	LESSON TITLE	SUPPLIES
Day 1	Bible Lesson	Paul and Silas Choose Joy	None
Day 2	Read-Aloud	Best-Case Scenario: "Cheertastic"	3 Sets of pompoms
Day 3	Giving Lesson	Get Together	1 Wagon
Day 4	Academy Lab	Let 'Er Flow	3/4 Cup baking soda, 1 Cup white vinegar, Several pounds of damp sand, 1 Small can, 1 Pitcher, 1 Container of red food coloring, 1 Tray
Day 5	Game Time	Pancake Toss	2 Bike helmets, 2 Solid-plastic plates, 10-15 Pancakes, Glue, Upbeat music (optional)
Bonus	Activity Page	Paul and Silas Coloring Page	1 Copy for each child

Lesson Introduction:

Adults often assume kids aren't under pressure. But, even in our great churches, families are going through struggles we don't always see. Just as the adults are trained, our kids must be trained to not be moved by what they see. They, too, can believe God, even when circumstances suggest doubt!

Faith is based on God's *good* plans for us (His Word). Circumstances can make us "feel" happy or sad—sometimes all in one day, or even in one hour! That's why we must have joy.

Joy is a powerful force not based on feelings (or flesh), which comes from our spirits in difficult situations. Even in the midst of crying over a challenging circumstance, joy can rise up from the inside. As we allow joy to rise up, the pressure of the difficulty will begin to lift, tears will ease, and we can turn our eyes to Jesus who is the One with all the answers (Psalm 121:1-2).

This week, as we study joy, understand that it is the force that makes way for faith to rise up. Then, peace will begin to work, as well. Pressure *can* make it difficult to walk by faith, but these fruit of the spirit are like a team of superheroes to the rescue!

Love,

Commander Kellie

Commander Kellie

Lesson Outline:

This week, you will teach your children about true, God-given joy. You will help them understand that joy is not only available when everything is going the way we want it to go, but real joy comes from knowing Jesus as Lord and Savior. It is a gift we can stir up, regardless of our circumstances, because we are God's redeemed, righteous children.

I. GOD WANTS US TO HAVE JOY, NO MATTER WHAT

a. God's nature is joyful! He wants His children to have the same joy He has. His joy is inside us when Jesus lives in our hearts.

b. Feeling happy is different from having joy on the inside.

c. Happiness isn't enough when a difficult situation happens.

II. THE JOY OF THE LORD IS OUR STRENGTH Nehemiah 8:10

a. When pressure comes, joy is *really* available. 1 Thessalonians 1:6

b. Jesus had joy when it seemed impossible to have it, even while He was hanging on a cross! Hebrews 12:2

c. Joy belongs to us, *especially in the hard times!*

d. The fruit of joy will help you stop feeling sad and sorry for yourself. A joyful Superkid can use his/her faith and come out a winner every time!

III. TALKING TO JESUS GETS OUR JOY ALL STIRRED UP Psalm 16:11

a. Greedy and evil men had Paul and Silas beaten and thrown into prison. Acts 16:22-26

b. The joy of the Lord showed up, and they chose to walk in it. They quit worrying about being in jail!

c. They had so much of the fruit of joy, they sang and praised God instead.

d. The fruit of joy will strengthen you more than enough to win any faith-fight!

Notes:_____

_____

_____

_____

_____

_____

_____

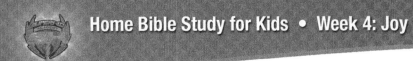

DAY 1: BIBLE LESSON

PAUL AND SILAS CHOOSE JOY

Memory Verse: Don't be dejected and sad, for the joy of the Lord is your strength! –Nehemiah 8:10b

(Corresponds with Lesson Outline No. I-III)

The world believes that joy comes when everything is right and wonderful in our lives. But as Christians, we know that we can have joy every day—regardless of our circumstances. Today's Bible lesson brings this point home. Paul and Silas were in a terrible place, but even there, they chose joy, and when joy shows up, miracles can happen!

Read Acts 16:22-26:
Paul and Silas in Prison

A mob quickly formed against Paul and Silas, and the city officials ordered them stripped and beaten with wooden rods. They were severely beaten, and then they were thrown into prison. The jailer was ordered to make sure they didn't escape. So the jailer put them into the inner dungeon and clamped their feet in the stocks.

Around midnight Paul and Silas were praying and singing hymns to God, and the other prisoners were listening. Suddenly, there was a massive earthquake, and the prison was shaken to its foundations. All the doors immediately flew open, and the chains of every prisoner fell off!

Discussion Questions:

1. **Do you think this was a good, fun day for Paul and Silas?**

   No, of course not! They were beaten and thrown into prison.

2. **How did they respond?**

   They began praying and singing hymns to God.

3. **The Bible says that "the other prisoners were listening." What do you think those prisoners were thinking?**

   Answers will vary. The prisoners may have been enjoying the singing, especially in such a dark and hopeless place, or they may have been in awe of Paul and Silas' faith, or they may have been listening to the words in the songs and receiving ministry from those words. Some may have even accepted Jesus through those songs.

4. **What happened as Paul and Silas were singing?**

   There was an earthquake. The doors flew open and the chains flew off the prisoners.

5. What can we learn from this passage?

Answers will vary.

Variation: Video

Many videos are available on this passage. Check online or the children's DVDs at your local library to find one.

Notes:_____

_____

_____

_____

_____

_____

_____

_____

_____

_____

_____

_____

_____

_____

_____

_____

_____

_____

_____

_____

_____

_____

_____

_____

_____

_____

DAY 2: READ-ALOUD

BEST-CASE SCENARIO: "CHEERTASTIC"

 Suggested Time: 15 minutes

 Memory Verse: Don't be dejected and sad, for the joy of the Lord is your strength! –Nehemiah 8:10b

Supplies: ■ 3 Sets of pompoms

(Corresponds with Lesson Outline No. II)

Background:

Today's read-aloud is based on a 2010 TV reality show "Worst-Case Scenario." It will highlight kids who encounter and overcome challenges by using the power of God and His Word.

Story:

"Welcome to 'Best-Case Scenario,'" said the narrator, standing just off to the side of the stage. "It's the show that looks at ordinary Christian kids in everyday situations. 'What's so exciting about that?' you might ask. Well, stick with us, and we'll show you.

"In a moment, we'll see an everyday challenge turn into a Best-Case Scenario. Now, let's meet our characters: Our first character is Mary. She is 14 years old and enjoys cheering, shopping and singing. Her favorite phrase is 'Go!'

"Our next character is Carrie. She is 15 years old, and she enjoys cheering, shopping and watching Disney Channel movies. Her favorite phrase is 'Fight!'

"And last, but not least, is Cherry. She is 14 years old and she enjoys cheering, shopping and telling jokes. Her favorite phrase is 'Win!'

"The theme of today's show is, J-O-Y. Can Mary, Carrie and Cherry overcome their personal obstacles before cheering at the state championship and keep their joy, no matter what? Let's find out."

Just then, the three contestants, Mary, Carrie and Cherry, entered from different sides of the stage, with their pompoms ready, to start stretching before the big game.

"Oh, my goodness!" said Mary. "I've had the best day!"

"Me, too!" Carrie agreed.

"Ditto!" Cherry called.

The three girls smiled at each other. "OK, so I thought my uniform was dirty, and it was like time to leave,"

Mary said, talking as much with her hands as she did with her mouth. "And, I'm like, OK, not cool, this is the state championship today. So, I go to the laundry room and guess what's hanging there all cleaned and ironed?"

"That cute, little, pink shirt with the polka dots?" Cherry offered.

"No, my uniform!" Mary said emphatically.

With that, all the girls squealed in delight.

"Hold on!" Carrie said, holding out both hands as if to stop the commotion. "You know how my mouth gets like really dry when I cheer?"

"Yeah?" both asked at once.

"Well, I was so nervous about the championship that I forgot my purse," Carrie explained. "And this kid just walks up to me and gives me $2 for a sports drink. Can you say, 'Cool'?"

"Cool!" Mary and Cherry nodded in agreement.

"Listen to this," Cherry spoke up. "I hurt my knee doing a handspring, and so this morning, I'm like, 'Lord, this *sooo* needs to be healed.' And look…" She ran across the stage and gracefully landed a round-off, back handspring as naturally as she ever had.

"Handspring!" Cherry pointed and cheered.

"This day is like *totally* cheertastic," Mary said before she jumped into a perfectly executed toe-touch.

"God is soooo amazing!" Carrie said. "No wonder Paul and Silas busted a cheer when they got thrown into jail."

Mary thought a moment. "Ummm, I think they sang a song. But you know they totally would have made great cheerleaders."

"I didn't know they were tumblers! Cool. And my brother said cheerleaders weren't in the Bible!" Carrie smiled smugly.

"Well, I don't know if they could tumble, but they were full of joy!" Mary said, and then grabbed her pompoms. "Girls, I feel a cheer coming on. Ready, OK!" The other two girls ran to grab their pompoms and lined up next to her.

Before she could start the cheer, she stopped. "Wait a minute. What rhymes with joy?"

Suddenly, Cherry rattled off several words that rhymed with joy. "Toy, boy, soy, Roy…oi! Oi! We could do like an Australian cheer! Oi!?"

"I love it!" Mary said, her eyes wide with delight. "Ready?"

"Oi!" Carrie and Cherry chimed. The girls took their positions and began their new cheer.

"There you have it," the narrator broke in. "A Best-Case Scenario. Instead of letting life's troubles get them down, Mary, Carrie and Cherry kept their joy. They are learning how to be joyful about the little blessings in life. Besides, what are cheerleaders without excitement? And, to top it all off, their team won the state championship, *and* they got their pictures in the paper, labeling them 'Cheertastic.' Talk about a Best-Case Scenario. It just doesn't get much better than that!"

Discussion Questions:

Use these questions as conversation starters. Enjoy this time of conversation with your children.

1. These girls were very silly, but they handled stressful situations well. What did you think about their attitudes?

2. How did they respond when difficult things happened?

3. Have you ever faced a really frustrating or disappointing situation? Did you choose joy?

4. Parents, share a testimony of a challenging time when you had to choose joy instead of anger or frustration.

Variation: Drama

Have your children act out this story. They can develop their own costumes, find their own props, practice their lines and present the drama to your family in the evening.

Notes:

DAY 3: GIVING LESSON — GET TOGETHER

Suggested Time: 10 minutes

 Offering Scripture: *If two of you agree here on earth concerning anything you ask, my Father in heaven will do it for you.* —Matthew 18:19

 Supplies: ☐ 1 Wagon

(Corresponds with Lesson Outline No. II)

Lesson Instructions:

Can someone help me with this lesson? *(Have one of your children sit in the wagon, with his/her feet inside. Challenge your child to move from one side of the room, or yard, to the other without changing position in the wagon. Since this demonstration requires the impossible, be prepared for a humorous response!)*

This is not an easy task! Let's see if your brother (or sister) can help out. Now, this demonstration will be much easier when there is someone to pull you across the room. *(Allow kids to demonstrate.)* Without some help, it's very challenging for someone to move across the room without changing position in the wagon, isn't it? But, once there's a helper, it makes the activity much easier. Well, this demonstration is similar to what Jesus said in Matthew 18:19: "If two of you agree here on earth concerning anything you ask, my Father in heaven will do it for you."

What happened when our first volunteer tried to move on his/her own? Yes! It was very challenging to move. He/she needed help! God wants us to work together. It brings us joy to work together to help someone, and to do it with friends who love God, who will pray with you, and be with you through good and challenging times. So, if there's something you've asked God for and it's seemed a little challenging, consider asking a friend to help "push your wagon." You can joyfully believe God together!

Did you know giving is the same way? When we work together to give our time, talent and money to God, wonderful things can happen. God wants to use us to help His Church reach people who don't know how much Jesus loves them and are hurting—to share our joy with them so they can be joyful, too!

Let's do our part. Let's prepare our tithes and offerings for this week's service.

Notes:_____

_____

_____

_____

_____

DAY 4: ACADEMY LAB | **LET 'ER FLOW**

 Suggested Time: *10 minutes*

 Key Scripture: *Although great trouble accompanied the Word, you were able to take great joy from the Holy Spirit!—taking the trouble with the joy, the joy with the trouble.* –1 Thessalonians 1:6 MSG

Supplies: ☐ *3/4 Cup baking soda,* ☐ *1 Cup white vinegar,* ☐ *Several pounds of damp sand,* ☐ *1 Small can,* ☐ *1 Pitcher,* ☐ *1 Container of red food coloring,* ☐ *1 Tray*

(Corresponds with Lesson Outline No. III)

Prior to Lesson:

Consider trying this demonstration prior to the segment presentation. Place the damp sand on the tray in the shape of a volcano. Press the small can into the top of the volcano, leaving the top uncovered. Build the sand up around the can until it is hidden. Place the baking soda in the can. Mix the vinegar and food coloring in the pitcher prior to the segment demonstration for timesaving purposes. When it's time for the eruption, pour the vinegar mixture into the can of baking soda, and watch the lava flow!

Lesson Instructions:

Today, we are going to make our own volcano! First, we'll place this damp sand on the tray and form it into the shape of a volcano. Now, we'll place this small can in the middle of it and build the sand up around the can. This volcano is similar to the challenges we face. Some challenges may seem like a big volcano, standing between us and our joy.

Let's see what God's Word says about our response to the challenges (or mountains) we face. Our key scripture says we are to choose joy! *(Pour the vinegar and food coloring mixture into the baking soda in the can and allow it to "erupt" while sharing the rest of the lesson.)* When we choose to turn our attention away from our challenges or "volcanoes" and focus on God, His promises and how much He loves us, happiness and joy will bubble out of our hearts and completely cover the mountain of problems that seem so big. The fruit of joy comes from our relationship with God and walking in His presence. As we learn and experience just how big His love is for us, we won't be able to stop the joy overflow!

Notes:_____

_____

_____

_____

_____

DAY 5: GAME TIME

PANCAKE TOSS

Suggested Time: 10-12 minutes

Memory Verse: Don't be dejected and sad, for the joy of the Lord is your strength! –Nehemiah 8:10b

Supplies: ☐ 2 Bike helmets, ☐ 2 Solid-plastic plates, ☐ 10-15 Pancakes, ☐ Glue, ☐ Upbeat music to play during game (optional)

(Corresponds with Lesson Outline No. I)

Prior to Game:

Divide players into teams of 2. Prepare 2 "plate hats" by gluing a solid-plastic plate to the top of each bike helmet. Choose a player who will toss and a player who will catch for each team. Place team members about 10 feet apart.

Game Instructions:

When the music begins, the players who will toss can begin flipping pancakes to their hat-wearing teammate. Catchers will try to catch the pancakes on their plates without using their hands.

Game Goal:

The team with the most pancakes on their "catch plate," wins.

Final Word:

The joy of the Lord is expressed in many different ways. This simple and fun game can bring lots of laughter to the players and the spectators. Let's laugh more!

Variation No. 1: Smaller Group

If you don't have enough players to make multiple teams, have your children take turns catching, with you participating as the thrower for all teams. Use a stopwatch or timer to see how many pancakes each player can throw in a minute. The player with the most pancakes on his/her plate wins.

Variation No. 2: Free Hand

If you don't have a bike helmet or prefer not to glue a plate to the top of it, then have catchers hold the plate on their heads with both hands. The plate cannot leave a player's head, and his/her hands cannot leave the plate.

Notes:_____

_____

_____

_____

_____

_____

_____

_____

_____

_____

_____

_____

_____

_____

_____

_____

_____

_____

_____

_____

_____

_____

_____

_____

_____

_____

_____

ACTIVITY PAGE

PAUL AND SILAS COLORING PAGE

 Memory Verse: Don't be dejected and sad, for the joy of the Lord is your strength! —Nehemiah 8:10b

(Corresponds with Lesson Outline No. III)

This week you learned how Paul and Silas reacted when they were thrown into prison. Enjoy coloring this scene of that miraculous event.

Notes:

WEEK 5: PEACE

Memory Verse: Then you will experience _God's peace_, which exceeds anything we can understand. His peace will guard your hearts and minds as you live in Christ Jesus. —Philippians 4:7

WEEK 5: SNAPSHOT

PEACE

DAY	TYPE OF LESSON	LESSON TITLE	SUPPLIES
Day 1	Bible Lesson	Jesus Calms the Storm	None
Day 2	Read-Aloud	Superkid Academy Worldwide: China	Images of China—The Great Wall, Terra-cotta army, Chinese countryside in various parts of China, Chinese food, cities (Beijing, Hong Kong, Shanghai, etc.), Chinese people, Forbidden City, the Summer Palace in Beijing, and in Jiuzhaigou Sichuan, the Giant Panda Breeding Research Base
Day 3	Giving Lesson	A Good Thing to Remember	A bag containing 10-20 miscellaneous items: (ex: a hairbrush, dog collar, pencil, baseball, etc.), A table to display the bag contents, A stopwatch (or a watch with a second hand)
Day 4	Food Fun	Nothing Missing	For each child: A few slices of deli meat, 2 Pieces of sliced cheese, 1 Slice of tomato, 2 Pieces of leaf lettuce, Mustard
Day 5	Game Time	Baby Crawl	8 Bibs, 8 Large diapers, 2 Rattles, 4 Sets of kneepads, 2 Cones (or tape), Upbeat music to play during the game (optional)
Bonus	Activity Page	Peace Color-By-Number	1 Copy for each child

Lesson Introduction:

Peace is a wonderful force for children to understand and put to use! It can help, along with joy, in a difficult situation. Just like Jesus in Mark 4:36-39, you can have supernatural calm in the middle of a storm. No matter what chaos is happening on the outside, you can still have a God-given sense of order on the inside.

The other aspect I like to teach the kids in this lesson has to do with being led by the Spirit. We can teach them to check their hearts to see what peace is saying to them. If we follow peace, we will let it "rule," or make decisions. For example, should we go to a friend's house? Should we watch a certain thing on TV or on the Internet? Do we hang out with this person or that person? What powerful wisdom is available to your Superkid when he/she learns to check his/her heart and follow the peace of God!

Love,

Commander Kellie

Commander Kellie

Lesson Outline:

Peace is a supernatural fruit that should rule our hearts and minds. This week, as you and your children study peace, remind them that real peace isn't driven by exterior forces. It is a fruit that fills us when we submit to the Holy Spirit.

I. JESUS AND HIS DISCIPLES WERE IN A GREAT STORM
Mark 4:36-39

    a. The storm was so fierce, the disciples became afraid for their lives.

    b. Jesus had so much peace, He was taking a wonderful nap.

    c. Jesus commanded the weather to be at peace, and everything became calm.

    d. The disciples let the storm control them. Jesus let peace control Him.

II. PEACE IS SUPERNATURAL FRUIT

    a. When Jesus let the peace of God inside Him come out, it stopped the storm.

    b. Sometimes tough circumstances feel like great storms.

    c. With God's peace, we have everything we need, with nothing missing! Philippians 4:7

III. WITH THE HOLY SPIRIT IN CHARGE, PEACE RULES OUR MINDS
Romans 8:6

    a. Jesus gave us His very own peace to use. John 14:27

    b. He instructed us to not allow our hearts to be troubled or afraid.

    c. Let His peace rule in your heart like a king—it's in charge! Colossians 3:15

Notes:_____

_____

_____

_____

_____

_____

_____

_____

_____

DAY 1: BIBLE LESSON — JESUS AND THE STORM

Memory Verse: Then you will experience God's peace, which exceeds anything we can understand. His peace will guard your hearts and minds as you live in Christ Jesus. —Philippians 4:7

(Corresponds with Lesson Outline No. I-II)

This week's Bible lesson shows us how we should respond when difficulties arise. Instead of giving in to fear, Jesus shows us how we are to let peace rule our hearts. Regardless of the situation, we can rest, knowing that God is always with us—He will *never* leave us nor forsake us (Hebrews 13:5).

Read Mark 4:35-41:
Jesus Calms the Storm

As evening came, Jesus said to his disciples, "Let's cross to the other side of the lake." So they took Jesus in the boat and started out, leaving the crowds behind (although other boats followed). But soon a fierce storm came up. High waves were breaking into the boat, and it began to fill with water.

Jesus was sleeping at the back of the boat with his head on a cushion. The disciples woke him up, shouting, "Teacher, don't you care that we're going to drown?"

When Jesus woke up, he rebuked the wind and said to the waves, "Silence! Be still!" Suddenly the wind stopped, and there was a great calm. Then he asked them, "Why are you afraid? Do you still have no faith?"

The disciples were absolutely terrified. "Who is this man?" they asked each other. "Even the wind and waves obey Him!"

Discussion Questions:

1. **Where were Jesus and the disciples when this storm began?**

   They were in a boat on a big lake.

2. **Why were the disciples so afraid?**

   The wind was blowing really hard and water was coming into the boat. The disciples were afraid they would drown.

3. **What did the disciples do when they became afraid?**

   They hurried to awaken Jesus, who was sleeping in the back of the boat.

4. **What did Jesus do when He woke up?**

   He rebuked, or scolded, the storm and told the waves to "be still."

5. **What happened next?**

The storm stopped.

6. **What did Jesus say to the disciples when He saw how scared they were?**

He asked them why they were afraid and had no faith.

7. **This week we're learning about peace. What can we learn from this passage about peace in Jesus?**

Peace is a supernatural fruit. Jesus was not affected by the storm because He had so much peace inside Him. In fact, He had so much peace, that the storm had to obey Him when He told it to stop. Since we are in Christ, we also have the ability to remain calm in difficult times and let peace calm our difficult situations, too. With the Holy Spirit in charge, peace will rule our minds.

Notes:_____

_____

_____

_____

_____

_____

_____

_____

_____

_____

_____

_____

_____

_____

_____

_____

_____

_____

_____

_____

_____

_____

_____

_____

DAY 2: READ-ALOUD

SUPERKID ACADEMY WORLDWIDE: CHINA

 Suggested Time: 15 minutes

 Memory Verse: Then you will experience God's peace, which exceeds anything we can understand. His peace will guard your hearts and minds as you live in Christ Jesus. —Philippians 4:7

Supplies: ■ Images of China: The Great Wall, Terra-cotta army, Chinese countryside in various parts of China, Chinese food, Cities (Beijing, Hong Kong, Shanghai, etc), Chinese people, Forbidden City, Summer Palace in Beijing, Giant Panda Breeding Research Base in Jiuzhaigou Sichuan

Background:

This week's Superkid Academy Worldwide read-aloud adventure takes you and your children to the People's Republic of China, where they will sample some of the beauty and amazement of China, and learn how to pray for Chinese Christians who are forced to meet in hidden churches.

Story:

There is a a huge wall that is so long, it appears to go on forever. It wraps across the countryside, going up over snowcapped mountaintops and running down through misty green valleys. It was built over 2,000 years ago, and was measured to be over 5500 miles long, 15-30 feet wide and approximately 25 feet tall. It is wide enough for two cars to drive on, side by side.[1]

It's called the Great Wall of China. And it's where we find our brave, but sometimes bumbling newsman, Steve Storyberg, reporting LIVE for all the world to see.

"Oh, man! I'm so tired. Whew! Out of breath. I feel like I've been walking for years. My feet are tired doggies, yelping for cold water."

"Steve!" says Kathleen Connery in a loud whisper. She has produced Steve's newscast for over 25 years. She's used to this by now. She tries again to get his attention, waving her arms. "Steve! You're on the air!"

"Yeah, I do need some air! I'm more tired than a snail in a Nascar race; more tired than a jellyfish at a water park; more tired than a mosquito on a…"

Suddenly, a bucket of water splashes onto Steve's face, wetting down his hair, his dark coat, his red tie and his tennis shoes. But, it works! Steve's attention is now centered on the broadcast!

"Oh, pardon me, ladies and gentlemen, I've never sneezed like that in my entire life. Hello, I'm Steve Storyberg, and this is Superkid Academy Worldwide News, coming to you super LIVE from the super country of China."

---

1   "The Great Wall Facts for Kids," *The Great Wall of China,* http://www.great-wallofchina.com/the-great-wall-of-china-facts-for-kids.html.

Producer Kathleen Connery, soundman George Lupas and cameraman Harrison Borg breathe a sigh of relief, all at the same time. It's not easy producing a LIVE TV show on location. But it helps to have a bucket of cold water nearby.

"It's true," Steve continues. "I've been walking on the Great Wall for two days now, and still haven't come to the end of it. It seems to have no ending, and no beginning. But of course, only our amazing God has no beginning and no ending!"

Kathleen counts down quietly and then points to a monitor that shows a long shot of a farmer in his field, working with a shovel. "Speaking of beginnings, right here in China in 1974, a farmer like this one was digging a well and unearthed some bits of what he thought were ceramic pots. But when Chinese archeologists came out to dig farther, they uncovered the famous Terra-Cotta Soldiers!"[2]

The monitor cuts to an army of thousands of hardened terra-cotta (clay), full-sized soldier statues, each with unique facial features, lined up in ranks. They were created around the third century B.C.—or about 300 years before Jesus was born.

"Those guys have been standing around for a long time. They must be hungry! And when you're hungry, it's nice to uncover a delicious dish of Chinese food, which I rather enjoy, myself."

As planned, Steve sits down to a table piled high with all kinds of Chinese food. He picks up his fork, hovering it over each plate.

"Wow, where to begin, huh? The lemon chicken, sweet and sour pork, fried rice with soy sauce, Chinese soup dumplings, crab meat rangoo…"

But before he can dig the fork into the treasures, George wrenches it from his hand, and replaces it with chopsticks.

"Ah, yes, the traditional Chinese wooden chopsticks. I'm a master at these. I can even do this!" Steve attempts the famous spinning chopsticks trick. But instead of that happening…

The sticks fly out of his hands. One shoots like a spear into Kathleen's hair and the other flips across the table, popping into the soy sauce, splattering George's white shirt, and then flipping a dumpling into Harrison's wide-open mouth! Surprised, Harrison chews and swallows with great delight.

"I'm a little rusty with the sticks, I guess.

"China is the most populous nation in the world, with 1.3 billion—20 percent of the world's population—living in one of the largest countries of the world, covering over 9.5 million square miles! Its capital is Beijing, home to nearly 11 million people! The languages they speak are Chinese (Mandarin), Cantonese and other dialects and minority languages. This nation has a wide variety of hills, plains and river deltas in the eastern part. But there are even deserts, high plateaus and mountains in the western part. China's climate has a lot of variety, too. It ranges from hot and tropical in the southern part (Hainan), to *really* cold, subarctic places in northeastern China (Manchuria).[3] China is certainly a place of many contrasts!

"China also has one of the fastest-growing economies in the world and in 2003, became the third nation (after the United States and Russia) to launch a manned spaceflight. They even plan to put a man on the moon sometime in the near future![4]

2   "Terra-Cotta Army Protects First Emperor's Tomb," John Roach, *National Geographic,* http://science.nationalgeographic.com/science/archaeology/emperor-qin/ (7/10/2013).

3   "China Facts," National Geographic Society, http://travel.nationalgeographic.com/travel/countries/china-facts/ (78/1/13).

4   "China Facts."

"Some great places to visit would be the Forbidden City and the Summer Palace in Beijing, and in Jiuzhaigou Sichuan, the Giant Panda Breeding Research Base.

"But now," Steve looks at the monitor, seeing rows and rows of small Chinese houses, packed tightly together. Yet he knows he is supposed to be seeing something else. "Um, ladies and gentlemen, excuse me."

Steve looks at Kathleen, ready to ask, "Where's the church building?"

But Kathleen is not in her place. She is standing right next to him, ready to share the broadcast, microphone in hand, and the wet chopstick removed from her hair.

"Thank you, Steve. Ladies and gentlemen, here you see a typical Chinese church."

Steve interrupts. "Um, excuse me Kathleen, but I don't see a church anywhere. Just houses."

"That's right, Steve, that's the point. You're not supposed to see the church. Just the houses. Since 1949, many Christians who have not wanted to join the government-sanctioned churches in China have been forced to meet secretly—not in church buildings—but in houses. These churches have come to be known as 'house churches.'"

Steve grows quiet. "I see. Or, well, I don't see. But why? We can worship in churches where everybody can see us. We could even pray or sing on a street corner if we wanted to."

The monitor shows a picture of some Chinese people being taken away by other Chinese people in uniforms.

"It's sad, Steve. Many of these Christians have been caught in the act of worshiping or reading their Bibles in what their government calls "illegal" and "unregistered" house churches. Many have been punished or have had to pay large amounts of money. So, they meet secretly, in the house churches."[5]

"We don't realize how blessed we are," Steve says thoughtfully, "to be able to worship when and wherever we want to."

"Steve," Kathleen answers, "we need to pray for them. Research has shown that over 100 million Chinese Christians meet in house churches.[6] This makes these Chinese believers one of the largest Christian populations in the world! Let's keep praying that God will protect and strengthen them, and draw more and more people in their country to receive Jesus as their Lord and Savior and follow Him. Even if they are having challenges, these Christians have great faith and joy in Jesus and expect victory in Him."

"Ahhh," says Steve, "just like the Great Wall of China here that seems to go on forever, these Christians' faith in Jesus will take them to heaven that really will go on forever and ever!"

Steve looks over and notices George, who has taken over Kathleen's role. He is using the chopstick from her hair to signal the end of the broadcast. Steve snaps back into news mode, and wraps it up.

"So tonight, ladies and gentlemen, as you eat your Lemon Chicken, or well, even a simple bowl of Chinese Noodle Soup, remember the great country of China and our brothers and sisters in the Chinese house churches. Pray for their protection, joy and strength in Jesus."

5   "How China Plans to Wipe Out House Churches," *Christianity Today,* Feb. 2013, http://www.christianitytoday.com/ct/2013/february-web-only/how-china-plans-to-wipe-out-house-churches.html (7/10/2013).

6   "Chinese Christians Face Tense Easter in Beijing," Calum MacLeod, *USA Today*, April, 2011, http://usatoday30.usatoday.com/news/world/2011-04-21-China-Christians-Easter.htm (7/10/2013); "Chinese House Church Leaders Meet With Gov't Officials," *One News Now-American Family News Network,* January 30, 2009, http://onenewsnow.com/church/2009/01/30/chinese-house-church-leaders-meet-with-govt-officials#.Udw_w6zheH1 (8/1/2013).

Kathleen looks over at Steve, expecting his famous sign-off saying. But when she notices a tear in his eye, she decides to sign off for both of them.

"This is Kathleen Connery, and Steve Storyberg, Superkid Academy Worldwide News."

Steve sniffs loudly, blows his nose and smiles.

Discussion Questions:

1. In your own words, explain why millions of Chinese Christians choose to worship in house churches.
2. How does that make you feel about going to your church?
3. How should people be praying for Chinese Christians?
4. How many of Steve's Chinese dinners can you remember?
5. Tell about a time when you and your family ate Chinese food.

Variation No. 1: Reading

Visit your local library to borrow books about China. Read them throughout the week.

Variation No. 2: Oral Report

For older children, have them research the history of Christianity in China and report to your family what they learn. Have them answer these questions:

- How were Christians treated in the past? Why were they treated like that?
- How are Christians treated today? If it is changing, why?
- Has the church grown larger or smaller as a result?
- What does the church in China look like?
- How can we pray for our Christian brothers and sisters in China?

Variation No. 3: Map Skills

Print a blank map of China from the Internet. Have your children mark the capital (Beijing), other large cities, major rivers, bordering countries and neighboring bodies of water. Have your children trace this map several times throughout the week to help them remember and gain better understanding of China.

Variation No. 4: International Food

To help your children learn more about China, consider visiting a Chinese restaurant or serving Chinese food for dinner.

Notes:

DAY 3: GIVING LESSON

A GOOD THING TO REMEMBER

Suggested Time: 10 minutes

 Offering Scripture: Remember the Lord your God. He is the one who gives you power to be successful. —Deuteronomy 8:18a

Supplies: ■ A bag containing 10-20 miscellaneous items: (ex: a hairbrush, dog collar, pencil, baseball, etc.), ■ A table to display bag contents, ■ A stopwatch (or a watch with a second hand)

(Corresponds with Lesson Outline No. II, III)

Lesson Instructions:

A good memory is important. Have you ever forgotten something?

Maybe you had a test you needed to study for, you got to school and were reminded that, uh-oh, you spent last night playing instead of reviewing your notes. Today, I have a little test of my own that I would like to try out. Will you help me with this test?

This is how my test works: In just a minute I am going to pour this bag out onto the table. You will have 90 seconds to look at all the things that were in the bag before I put them back. Let's see how many of those things you can remember. Are you ready? Here we go! (Dump items on the table and begin your timer. Count down the last 10 seconds and gather items back into the bag.) Now, let's see how good your memory is. Can you tell me what is in this bag? *(Take items out as your helper names them.)*

Was it a little tough remembering everything you had seen? You did a great job. Thank you for helping me! You know, remembering things that are in a bag is not really a big deal, but there *are* some things that are a big deal to remember. Here's one in God's Word, in Deuteronomy 8:18: "Remember the Lord your God. He is the one who gives you power to be successful." That verse is letting us know that we should never forget where the good things in our lives really come from—from our God who is always helping us!

How Is God Helping Us?

He helps our family to be healthy, happy and at peace. He helps you in your schoolwork and makes sure we all have food to eat and clothes to wear. He gives us His peace to use, and helps us to not allow our hearts to be troubled or afraid. With His peace ruling in our hearts, we have everything we need, with nothing missing, nothing broken.

Can you think of other ways God helps us? *(Allow children to share and discuss their answers.)*

Wow, when you think about it, those are great things to remember. When we remember God, it makes our hearts happy, and we want to give something to the One who is always there for us—the One who gives us everything we need to be successful...OUR GOD!

When God gives us so much, is it really hard to give back to Him? When we give our tithe, offering, talent or time, it's a way we can give back to God. Those are ways we show Him how much we love Him. Let's prepare our offering for this week's church service, now.

Notes:_____

_____

_____

_____

_____

_____

_____

_____

_____

_____

_____

_____

_____

_____

_____

_____

_____

_____

_____

_____

_____

_____

_____

_____

_____

_____

_____

_____

DAY 4: FOOD FUN

NOTHING MISSING

 Suggested Time: 5-8 minutes

 Key Scripture: I am leaving you with a gift—peace...." (<u>Peace</u> means nothing missing or broken.)
—John 14:27

 Teacher Tip: Plan to use this lesson during one lunch or dinner, and feel free to increase the supplies so each of your children can participate.

Supplies: For each child: ■ A few slices of deli meat, ■ 2 Pieces of sliced cheese, ■ 1 Slice of tomato, ■ 2 Pieces of leaf lettuce, ■ Mustard

(Corresponds with Lesson Outline No. II)

Prior to Lesson:

Display the sandwich supplies on the table.

The bread has been purposely omitted from the supplies to challenge your child in this sandwich-making activity.

Allow your children to start making the sandwich and then discover the missing ingredient, bread.

Lesson Instructions:

I know you know how to make a sandwich, AND that you're very hungry! OK, here are the things you need. Go ahead and make your sandwich. Put whatever you'd like on it. And as soon as you're finished, we'll give thanks to the Lord and you can eat it. *(Your children may try to make a sandwich without bread. It will be messy and funny to watch.)*

What's wrong? I thought you said you knew how to make a sandwich! If I were as hungry as you are, I'd quit messing around and make my sandwich. Why aren't you doing what I asked? Please make the sandwich. *(Your children will finally explain the problem.)*

Oh, I see! Without bread there is no sandwich. Why didn't you say so in the first place? A sandwich isn't a sandwich without the bread. Of course! I knew something was missing....

But, what does peace have to do with things missing? Good question. Well, the kind of peace God gives—from the Hebrew word *shalom*—means nothing is missing or broken. This sandwich was missing something pretty important, and it definitely made things less than peaceful, wouldn't you say? It is certainly messy and crazy trying to make a sandwich when there is no bread! Not to mention, it's much less filling!

With God's kind of peace, you'll always have what you need, no missing ingredients, or broken parts. So, the next time you're making a sandwich, remember to thank God for giving you His kind of peace, which means you'll never be missing your bread or anything else you need!

Notes:

_____

_____

_____

_____

_____

_____

_____

_____

_____

_____

_____

_____

_____

_____

_____

_____

_____

_____

_____

_____

_____

_____

_____

_____

_____

_____

_____

_____

_____

_____

DAY 5: GAME TIME

BABY CRAWL

 Suggested Time: 10 minutes

 Memory Verse: Then you will experience _God's peace_, which exceeds anything we can understand. His peace will guard your hearts and minds as you live in Christ Jesus. –Philippians 4:7

Supplies: ☐ 8 Bibs, ☐ 8 Large diapers, ☐ 2 Rattles, ☐ 4 Sets of kneepads, ☐ 2 Cones (or 2 tape lines on the floor for finish-line markers), ☐ Upbeat music to play during the game (optional)

(Corresponds with Lesson Outline No. II, III)

Prior to Game:

Divide players into 2 teams. Have all players place bibs, diapers and kneepads over their existing clothes. The 2 teams will line up next to each other, on their hands and knees, at the starting line. The first 2 "babies" in line will each hold a rattle. Place a cone or tape marker for the finish line.

Game Instructions:

This will be a relay race. The players will start when they hear, "Go, baby!" The first 2 "babies" will crawl to the finish-line marker and back while holding their rattles. As the first babies return, they'll shout, "Whaaah!" and pass their rattle to the next baby in line. While their teammate is crawling, the first babies will give their kneepads to the third baby.

Game Goal:

The first team to complete the crawl relay, wins.

Final Word:

Ask your children if they can remember when they were babies, crawling and crying and wearing a diaper. Hopefully, no one can! Ask if it would seem odd if they were to crawl into church with a diaper and a rattle each week.

What if you walked into church and your leaders were wearing diapers and crying for snack time? Have you considered that this is what God sees daily with many Christians? Sometimes He sees very old and very silly babies with their diapers needing to be changed. When we don't allow the fruit of the spirit on the inside of us to come out on the outside of us, then we will be acting like spiritual babies—trying to get our own way, being selfish, feeling sorry for ourselves and full of fear. But when we allow love, joy, peace and the other fruit of the spirit to come out of us, we are growing up in Him! Let's make sure we grow up God's way and forget about wearing diapers all our lives!

Variation No. 1: Simple Race

If you only have 2 players, change the race to 1 player per team. You could even make each player complete the course 2-3 times!

Variation No. 2: Party Game

Consider inviting other families to participate in this game, perhaps for a party, co-op game time or multiple family game night.

Notes:_____

_____

_____

_____

_____

_____

_____

_____

_____

_____

_____

_____

_____

_____

_____

_____

_____

_____

_____

_____

_____

_____

_____

_____

_____

ACTIVITY PAGE

PEACE COLOR-BY-NUMBER

Memory Verse: Then you will experience <u>God's peace</u>, which exceeds anything we can understand. His peace will guard your hearts and minds as you live in Christ Jesus. —Philippians 4:7

(Corresponds with Lesson Outline No. I)

This week, you've learned about the God-kind of peace. Complete this color-by-number to show an example from the Bible of this kind of peace in action.

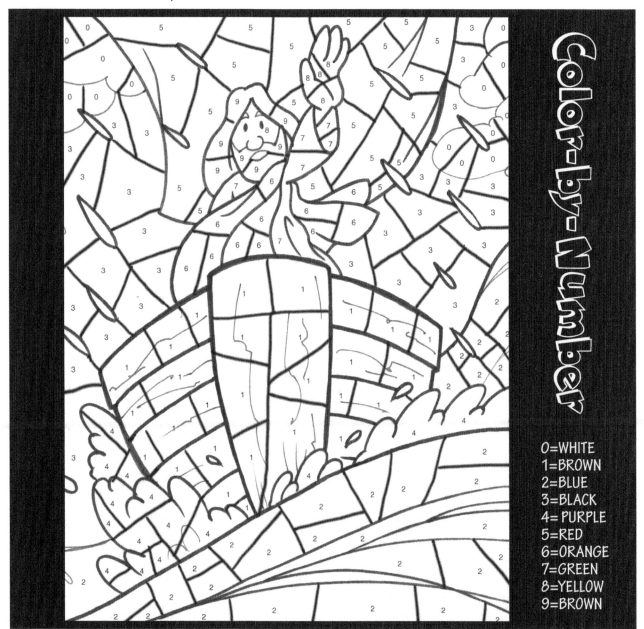

Color-by-Number

0=WHITE
1=BROWN
2=BLUE
3=BLACK
4= PURPLE
5=RED
6=ORANGE
7=GREEN
8=YELLOW
9=BROWN

WEEK 6: PATIENCE

 Memory Verse: Be assured and understand that the trial and proving of your faith bring out endurance and steadfastness and patience. —James 1:3 AMP

WEEK 6: SNAPSHOT

PATIENCE

DAY	TYPE OF LESSON	LESSON TITLE	SUPPLIES
Day 1	Bible Lesson	Abraham's Promise	None
Day 2	Food Fun	Dip Into Patience	1 1-Quart crockpot, 1 Double boiler or mixing bowl (preferably tempered glass or metal) placed on top of a pan of simmering water, 1 Butter knife, 1 Can opener, Measuring spoons, Cutting board, Power cord, Toothpicks or thin wooden skewers, 2 Ounces unsweetened baking chocolate (chopped), 18 Ounces semisweet chocolate (chopped), 14-Ounce can sweetened condensed milk, 1/2 Teaspoon vanilla, 4 Ounces white chocolate (finely chopped), Suggested dipping items: cookies, pound-cake squares, brownies, strawberries, marshmallows and/or apples
Day 3	Giving Lesson	Keep Your Faith On	1 Teakettle, 1 Pitcher of water, 1 Tea bag, 1 Cup and saucer, 1 Hot plate
Day 4	Object Lesson	Servant Challenge	5 Envelopes, Notecards, Signature slips
Day 5	Game Time	Donut Fishing	1 Dowel rod (per team of 2), 1 Roll of white twine, 1 Package of plastic clothespins, 1 Glazed donut per player
Bonus	Activity Page	Abraham's Journey (Maze)	1 Copy for each child

Lesson Introduction:

I like to ask kids what kinds of things require patience. Basically, their answers will fall into two categories: patience with people and patience when using their faith. They seem so different, but the key to walking in patience is realizing that they require the same patience!

We know we need to be patient while believing God for something, but we don't use one kind of patience for that and another kind while waiting for mom to fix dinner! The secret to building up our patience (like a body-builder builds a muscle) is to _exercise_ it as we wait for dinner! They don't seem connected, but it is the same force inside needed for both instances.

People tend to get more impatient with family than with anyone else. This is a great time to encourage your Superkids to be patient with Mom, Dad and siblings—waiting for dinner, riding in the car ("Are we there yet?"), interacting with younger brothers and sisters. In all these things, we can exercise the force of patience, so when we need it in a faith fight, it's strong and developed!

By the way, I love messages that allow me, as Commander, to give some "Home Improvement" help and partner with you, the parents, to help raise some awesome Superkids!

Love,

Commander Kellie

Commander Kellie

Lesson Outline:

This week, you will study Abraham. What an excellent lesson in patience his life was! From the time that he first answered God's call to the moment his son, Isaac, was born, 25 years passed. Talk about patience!

Society tells us that we should have what we want when we want it. We're taught that this kind of thought is efficient, but God works according to spiritual laws that have nothing to do with this fast-food mentality. Encourage your children to slow down and reflect on God's work in their lives. Then share your experiences that required patience. Let this be a time of training for the work God calls them to in the future.

I. PATIENCE SHOWS OUR TRUST IN GOD

a. We live in a very impatient world. People want everything in a hurry—right now!

b. When we're patient, we are letting God work out our lives.

c. God's Word gives the hope and encouragement our patience needs. Romans 15:4-5

d. If we allow it, patience works perfectly to make us complete. James 1:4

II. GOD WANTS US TO BE PATIENT WITH ONE ANOTHER
Colossians 3:12-13

a. There are times when we need to be patient with our families.

b. Sometimes, the people closest to us are the easiest to be impatient with.

c. The Bible tells us to be understanding of each other's faults. Ephesians 4:2

III. WE NEED THE FRUIT OF PATIENCE FOR OUR FAITH TO WORK
Hebrews 6:12

a. Abraham received amazing promises from God. Genesis 12:2

b. Without patience, Abraham's faith would have given up. Hebrews 6:15

c. We are to follow Abraham's example, and hold on to the promises of God.

d. Don't throw away your faith (trust). Follow it up with patience. It works! Hebrews 10:36

Notes:_____

_____

_____

_____

_____

DAY 1: BIBLE LESSON **ABRAHAM'S PROMISE**

 Memory Verse: *Be assured and understand that the trial and proving of your faith bring out endurance and steadfastness and patience.* –James 1:3 AMP

(Corresponds with Lesson Outline No. I, III)

This week's Bible lesson focuses on Abraham's life. You will read three different passages to your children so they can understand how long Abraham waited for the fulfillment of his promise from the Lord. His life was a great example of how God keeps His Word when we are patient.

Read Genesis 12:1-5, 17:1-8 and 21:1-6
The Call of Abram

The Lord had said to Abram, "Leave your native country, your relatives, and your father's family, and go to the land that I will show you. I will make you into a great nation. I will bless you and make you famous, and you will be a blessing to others. I will bless those who bless you and curse those who treat you with contempt. All the families on earth will be blessed through you."

So Abram departed as the Lord had instructed, and Lot went with him. Abram was seventy-five years old when he left Haran. He took his wife, Sarai, his nephew Lot, and all his wealth—his livestock and all the people he had taken into his household at Haran—and headed for the land of Canaan.

Abram Is Named Abraham

When Abram was ninety-nine years old, the Lord appeared to him and said, "I am El-Shaddai—'God Almighty.' Serve me faithfully and live a blameless life. I will make a covenant with you, by which I will guarantee to give you countless descendants."

At this, Abram fell face down on the ground. Then God said to him, "This is my covenant with you: I will make you the father of a multitude of nations! What's more, I am changing your name. It will no longer be Abram. Instead, you will be called Abraham, for you will be the father of many nations. I will make you extremely fruitful. Your descendants will become many nations, and kings will be among them!

"I will confirm my covenant with you and your descendants after you, from generation to generation. This is the everlasting covenant: I will always be your God and the God of your descendants after you. And I will give the entire land of Canaan, where you now live as a foreigner, to you and your descendants. It will be their possession forever, and I will be their God."

The Birth of Isaac

The Lord kept his word and did for Sarah exactly what he had promised. She became pregnant, and she gave birth to a son for Abraham in his old age. This happened at just the time God had said it would. And Abraham named their son Isaac. Eight days after Isaac was born, Abraham circumcised him as God had commanded. Abraham was 100 years old when Isaac was born.

Discussion Questions:

1. **How old was Abram when the Lord first promised that he would become "the father of many nations"?**

   He was 75 years old.

2. **How old was Abram when the Lord changed his name to Abraham?**

   He was 99 years old.

3. **How old was Abraham when his wife Sarah had a son?**

   He was 100 years old.

4. **How many years passed from the time that Abraham was first promised to be a father until the time it actually occurred?**

   Twenty-five years passed from the first time God told him he would become "the father of many nations" until Isaac was born.

5. **Parents, take this time to talk about the patience it required for Abraham to trust God for 25 years. Point out that Isaac was the reward for that patience.**

6. **Parents, share your own testimony of a time when you needed patience to succeed. How did God reward your patience and obedience?**

   Notes:_____

   _____

   _____

   _____

   _____

   _____

   _____

   _____

   _____

   _____

   _____

   _____

   _____

   _____

DAY 2: FOOD FUN

DIP INTO PATIENCE

 Suggested Time: 10 minutes

 Memory Verse: Be assured and understand that the trial and proving of your faith bring out endurance and steadfastness and patience. –James 1:3 AMP

 Teacher Tip: Cover the ingredients until it's time to reveal the CHOCOLATE! If your children are old enough, allow them to help you cut up the dipping items. If not, cut the dipping items prior to the lesson. Melt the chocolate in the double boiler or bowl over pan of simmering water ahead of time and keep it warm so it stays melted.

Ingredients: ☐ 2 Ounces unsweetened baking chocolate (chopped), ☐ 18 Ounces semisweet chocolate (chopped), ☐ 14-Ounce can sweetened condensed milk, ☐ 1/2 Teaspoon vanilla, ☐ 4 Ounces white chocolate (finely chopped), ☐ Suggested dipping items: cookies, pound-cake squares, brownies, strawberries, marshmallows and/or apples

Prior to Lesson: In the double boiler, or bowl over a simmering pan of water, combine 1/2 the ingredients: 1 ounce of baking chocolate, 9 ounces of semisweet chocolate and 1/2 the can of sweetened condensed milk.

Recipe:
1. Have the children combine the other 1/2 of the same ingredients in the crockpot, and mix well.
2. Cover and cook on LOW, stirring frequently, until the chocolate is melted (about one hour for the crockpot).
3. Stir well and add 1/2 the vanilla (1/4 teaspoon) to the crockpot.
4. Mix well.
5. Sprinkle the finely chopped white chocolate over the melted crockpot mixture.
6. Cover and cook in the crockpot 10-12 minutes more on LOW until the white chocolate is melted (less time for double boiler).
7. Stir gently so it makes a marbled effect.

Supplies: ☐ 1 1-Quart crockpot, ☐ 1 Double boiler or a mixing bowl (preferably tempered glass or metal) placed on top of a pan of simmering water, ☐ 1 Butter knife to cut dipping ingredients, ☐ 1 Can opener, ☐ Measuring spoons, ☐ Cutting board, ☐ Power cord, ☐ Toothpicks or thin wooden skewers

(Corresponds with Lesson Outline No. I)

Lesson Instructions:

Today, we are going to make something sweet we all enjoy eating.

Can anyone guess what the main ingredient is?

That's right—CHOCOLATE! There are two kinds, regular and white. *(Remove napkin to reveal ingredients.)*

Who likes the taste of chocolate more than anything else?

If your children are old enough, have them help you chop up the chocolate while you talk.

Talk about chocolate coming in many forms and colors—candy bars, chocolate syrup, chocolate morsels. But it is *really* good when it's melted and you can cover in chocolate some of your favorite things to eat! *(Make a big deal about how yummy things are covered in melted chocolate.)*

Ask your helpers to combine the baking chocolate, semisweet chocolate and the sweetened condensed milk, in the crock pot and mix well. Next, add the vanilla and white chocolate. Turn the power to LOW and put the lid on. Do you know what we are going to dip into our chocolate? Do you think you can handle a chocolate blessing this wonderful? Have your children use the butter knife and begin cutting the "dipping" items. When the cutting is finished, give your children the skewers and have them dip some goodies into the melted chocolate, covering them completely. *(They will quickly realize the chocolate is far from melted and there is no way they are going to be able to do what you ask.)*

Did you follow my instructions completely? *(Walk them through the steps again.)*

This time, point out that you forgot to add the last ingredient—PATIENCE! Should we throw out all the chocolate since it is not melted? Then, I think we will have to have patience when we are melting chocolate! If we melt it too fast, it will burn and taste really yucky. But, if we melt it slowly, at the right temperature, it will turn a plain marshmallow into a yummy treat.

Are you ready to use your patience and wait for it to melt so we can all share in the treat? This reminds me of what we've been learning about patience. Just as we will not give up and throw our yummy chocolate promise away, Abraham knew God had promised him big things, and he had to have the patience to walk it out, too. Abraham's faith was growing by leaps and bounds as his patience got a real workout! God's promise was fulfilled right on time.

(Uncover the already melted chocolate in the double boiler.) While we're waiting patiently for our crock pot chocolate, we can enjoy the taste of our yummy treat that I melted earlier in this pan. *(Add 1/4 teaspoon vanilla.)* Now, we'll gently stir in the white chocolate to create the marbled effect just before we serve it. The reason we add the white chocolate at the end is to remind us how faith and patience work when we add the two together. It creates something really cool, and then it's complete. Always remember: Don't throw away your faith—follow it up with patience…and some yummy dippers. IT WORKS!

Notes:_____

_____

_____

_____

_____

_____

_____

DAY 3: GIVING LESSON KEEP YOUR FAITH ON

 Suggested Time: 10 minutes

 Offering Scripture: But let patience have its perfect work, that you may be perfect and complete, lacking nothing. –James 1:4 NKJV

Supplies: ☐ 1 Teakettle, ☐ 1 Pitcher of water, ☐ 1 Tea bag, ☐ 1 Cup and saucer, ☐ 1 Hot plate

(Corresponds with Lesson Outline No. I)

Lesson Instructions:

Have you ever been to a tea party? Maybe you haven't, but you've probably seen someone make a cup of tea. Can anyone tell me what the first step in the tea-making process is? Correct! First, we'll pour water into the teakettle. Next, we'll turn the burner on and place the kettle on the burner. Have you ever noticed that it seems to take forever for water to boil when you're in a hurry? You might even get impatient, turn the burner off and walk away. But, will you ever get a cup of hot tea that way? No!

Do you realize that trusting God is just like making a cup of tea? When we give our offerings, it's like filling the kettle with water. When we use our faith and ask God for something we need, it's like turning on the burner. In order for the water to boil, the burner must stay on. In order for us to see the results we want, we'll have to keep our faith on. We can't allow ourselves to become impatient if it looks like nothing is happening. If we get impatient, it shuts off our faith! Instead, we need to turn our faith on "high." How can we do that? By thanking and praising God every day for taking care of us and supplying all our needs. Let's prepare our offering for this week's church service, now.

Notes:_____
_____
_____
_____
_____
_____
_____
_____
_____
_____
_____

DAY 4: OBJECT LESSON   SERVANT CHALLENGE

 Suggested Time: *10 minutes*

 Key Scripture: *And mark that you do this with humility and discipline...steadily, pouring yourselves out for each other in acts of love.* –Ephesians 4:2 MSG

 Teacher Tip: *Remember to reward your children next week if they complete this challenge.*

Supplies: ☐ *5 Envelopes,* ☐ *Notecards,* ☐ *Signature slips*

(Corresponds with Lesson Outline No. II)

Prior to Lesson:

Prepare 5 envelopes, each containing a notecard with a specific chore written on it that your children don't normally do (ex: washing the dishes, making someone's bed, taking out the trash, sweeping the porch or sidewalk, folding laundry). Place a signature slip inside each envelope. Sample wording for the signature slip could be: "I_____ confirm that my child cheerfully completed a full week of his/her task without any prompting." *(The line provided is for your signature.)*

Lesson Instructions:

Today is "Servant Challenge" day. If you would like to know what "Servant Challenge" is, listen to this scripture: "And mark that you do this with humility and discipline...steadily, pouring yourselves out for each other in acts of love" (Ephesians 4:2 MSG). I like the part that says, "steadily, pouring yourselves out for each other."

We're learning this week about being patient, and one great way to practice patience is by serving someone—doing things for them. We are going to do a little experiment over the next week. Do you think you could stick with something for a whole week? When we think about patience, it seems the hardest people to be patient with are our own family members—brothers and sisters or maybe moms and dads. And usually, family members are the ones who need our patience the most. This servant challenge is to help you grow in your patience for these very important people.

There are five sealed envelopes here. Inside each one, there is a special act of service written on a card that you will be doing each day for the next week. These chores are not your regular ones, but they are ones that will help someone else out. Now, here's the fun little extra I haven't told you about. There are actually TWO pieces of paper in these envelopes, one with your servant assignment and another one for me or your dad/mom to sign when you complete the chore with a great attitude. If you complete each chore and get each paper signed, you will receive a special treat. But, the best part of this challenge is that you'll be growing a big crop of "patience fruit" that our whole family will enjoy—what a treat for all of us!

Notes:_____

Series: Fruit of the Spirit

DAY 5: GAME TIME

DONUT FISHING

Suggested Time: 6-8 minutes

Memory Verse: Be assured and understand that the trial and proving of your faith bring out endurance and steadfastness and patience. –James 1:3 AMP

Supplies: ☐ 1 Dowel rod (per team of two), ☐ 1 Roll of white twine, ☐ 1 Package of plastic clothespins, ☐ 1 Glazed donut per player

(Corresponds with Lesson Outline No. I, II)

Prior to Game:

Create "fishing poles" from the above supplies: Tie the twine to 1 end of a dowel rod. Consider securing the twine with hot glue or tape to keep it from slipping. Tie the other end of the line to a clothespin.

Game Instructions:

Divide players into teams of 2—1 player to cast the "fishing" line, and 1 player to eat. Players should be a short distance away from each other, facing one another—1 standing and 1 kneeling. Attach a donut to the end of the line by using the clothespin on each player's fishing line. Teammates on the floor will clasp their hands behind their backs. If hands are used at any time to help eat the donut, that team will be disqualified. The goal is to eat as much of the donut as possible before the music stops. This game will be a challenge, so each team will require patience and teamwork. When the music begins, each player with a fishing pole will cast to his/her teammate. Signal to stop the music after a designated amount of time, then decide which team has eaten the most of its donut. If time allows, consider playing several rounds.

Game Goal:

Use patience and teamwork to eat the largest amount of donut from the fishing pole in a designated amount of time.

Final Word:

The sport of fishing and "fishing for people" with whom to share God's love requires patience. Fishing for people takes even more patience than water fishing for swimming fish, but it's even more fun. What a great way to practice this awesome fruit of the spirit!

Variation: Fewer Children

If you don't have enough children to create multiple teams, allow each child to take a turn eating and a turn casting.

Notes:
_____
_____
_____
_____
_____
_____
_____
_____
_____
_____
_____
_____
_____
_____
_____
_____
_____
_____
_____
_____
_____
_____
_____
_____
_____
_____
_____
_____
_____
_____
_____
_____

ACTIVITY PAGE

ABRAHAM'S JOURNEY

Memory Verse: Be assured and understand that the trial and proving of your faith bring out endurance and steadfastness and patience. —James 1:3 AMP

(Corresponds with Lesson Outline No. III)

When Abraham was 75 years old, God told him to leave his home in Haran to begin a journey that would end with him becoming the father of many nations. In this maze, help Abraham find his way from Haran to Isaac.

Notes:

WEEK 7: KINDNESS

Memory Verse: I, too, try to please everyone in everything I do. I don't just do what is best for me; I do what is best for others so that many may be saved. —1 Corinthians 10:33

WEEK 7: SNAPSHOT

KINDNESS

DAY	TYPE OF LESSON	LESSON TITLE	SUPPLIES
Day 1	Bible Lesson	Jesus Is Kindness	None
Day 2	Read-Aloud	Superkid Academy Worldwide: Spain	Images of Spain—Plaza de Toros de Las Ventas, castles, rivers, cities (Barcelona, Madrid, Toledo, etc.), Spanish countryside, Spanish food, people, Sagrada Familia, running of the bulls in Pamplona
Day 3	Giving Lesson	A Different Kind of Treasure	A treasure map, A treasure box (with old treasures inside)
Day 4	Object Lesson	Good Steering	A bridle and rope
Day 5	Game Time	Ping-Pong Gone Wrong	2 Aprons, 2 Packets of ping-pong balls, Masking tape, Upbeat music (optional)
Bonus	Activity Page	Good-Attitude Word Search	1 Copy for each child

Lesson Introduction:

In the next few weeks, the kids will begin to understand the difference between kindness, gentleness and goodness. These fruit of the spirit sound so much alike, but have very different functions.

Kindness is a great antidote to selfishness. You can't think about what you want or need when this fruit is in use. Kindness will cause Superkids to give their last cookie away, leave the best for someone else and incon-venience themselves to help others.

This is a great place to bring up your own personal testimonies of kindness shown through you and to you. Have your Superkids think of situations where kindness could be exercised. They may surprise you! Then, ask them about the potential results of showing kindness to their family and friends.

I like to issue a challenge for Superkids: Let kindness take the place of selfishness. Have Superkids declare to the Lord that they will walk in kindness and be a great representative of the Lord Jesus!

Love,

Commander Kellie

Commander Kellie

Lesson Outline:

When we exhibit the fruit of kindness, we are a blessing to those around us—to our family, friends, neighbors, co-workers and the Body of Christ. God is able to use us to show His love to others. This week, enjoy teaching your children about the importance of kindness and how they can stir it up in their lives to be ambassadors for the Lord.

I. KINDNESS: TO GO OUT OF YOUR WAY TO BE WHAT OTHERS NEED

a. When you choose kindness, the needs of others become more important.

b. Kindness is giving yourself or your time away (serving others).

c. It is the outside proof (fruit) that the Holy Spirit lives in us. 2 Corinthians 6:6

II. JESUS WAS FULL OF KINDNESS

a. Jesus kindly laid aside His place in heaven for the sake of others. Philippians 2:6-8

b. He is rich in kindness. Ephesians 1:7

c. We follow Jesus' example when we are kind to others. Ephesians 4:32

III. WE ARE JUST LIKE HIM

a. We are to live like Jesus here, in this world! 1 John 4:17

b. The ultimate expression of kindness is to lead people to Jesus. 1 Corinthians 10:33

c. Kindness keeps our minds off ourselves. You take care of others, and God will take care of you!

Notes:_____

_____

_____

_____

_____

_____

_____

_____

_____

_____

DAY 1: BIBLE LESSON   JESUS IS KINDNESS

 Memory Verse: I, too, try to please everyone in everything I do. I don't just do what is best for me; I do what is best for others so that many may be saved. —1 Corinthians 10:33

(Corresponds with Lesson Outline No. I-III)

The Bible encourages us to live as Jesus lived, to let His life be an example to us. The Apostle Paul gives us a clear picture of how the Lord wants us to live and by it, we can judge and adjust our own attitudes, so we can live in victory and in honor of our heavenly Father.

Read Philippians 2:1-11:
Have the Attitude of Christ

Is there any encouragement from belonging to Christ? Any comfort from his love? Any fellowship together in the Spirit? Are your hearts tender and compassionate? Then make me truly happy by agreeing wholeheartedly with each other, loving one another, and working together with one mind and purpose.

Don't be selfish; don't try to impress others. Be humble, thinking of others as better than yourselves. Don't look out only for your own interests, but take an interest in others, too.

You must have the same attitude that Christ Jesus had.

Though he was God, he did not think of equality with God as something to cling to. Instead, he gave up his divine privileges; he took the humble position of a slave and was born as a human being. When he appeared in human form, he humbled himself in obedience to God and died a criminal's death on a cross.

Therefore, God elevated him to the place of highest honor and gave him the name above all other names, that at the name of Jesus every knee should bow, in heaven and on earth and under the earth, and every tongue confess that Jesus Christ is Lord, to the glory of God the Father.

Discussion Questions:

1. **How would you describe the attitude of Jesus in this passage?**

   Answers will vary.

2. **What are some things that this passage tells us to do?**

   This passage tells us to walk in agreement with one another, love one another, work together in unity, be humble, think of others as better than ourselves and take an interest in others.

3. **Do you think that in His selfless and dedicated serving of others and loving them, Jesus had opportunities to not walk in the fruit of kindness?**

He was just like us, so He probably had many opportunities to be unkind and grumpy when He was tired or in other situations. But Jesus depended on the power of the fruit of kindness within Him. We must follow His example and do the same thing, always trusting our heavenly Father to help us be kind to others.

4. **What are some things that this passage tells us NOT to do?**

This passage tells us not to be selfish, try to impress others or look out for our own interests.

5. **How did Jesus live this?**

Jesus, God's Son, gave up His place in heaven to become a human so He could die for our sins.

6. **Do you know of anyone in your life who reflects the kindness Jesus did?**

Answers will vary, but remind your children of the kind people in their lives—parents, grandparents, pastors, teachers, neighbors and friends. Help them see the gospel in action around them.

7. **What are some practical ways we can live this passage?**

Answers will vary.

Variation: Catch Kindness

Throughout the week, point out acts of kindness you witness in others and in your child. When situations arise that give your child a choice between kindness and selfishness, encourage them to choose correctly, and then thank them when they do.

Notes:_____

_____

_____

_____

_____

_____

_____

_____

_____

_____

_____

_____

_____

_____

DAY 2: READ-ALOUD

SUPERKID ACADEMY WORLDWIDE: SPAIN

 Suggested Time: 15 minutes

 Key Scripture: *Beloved, let us love one another, for love is of God; and everyone who loves is born of God and knows God.* –1 John 4:7-8 NKJV

Supplies: ■ Images of Spain—Plaza de Toros de Las Ventas, castles, rivers, cities (Barcelona, Madrid, Toledo, etc.), Spanish countryside, Spanish food, people, Sagrada Familia, running of the bulls in Pamplona

Background:

This week, our Superkid Academy Worldwide read-aloud adventure zooms us across the globe to Spain, where we will meet Diego and Isabella, and see the amazing and unusual ways people are becoming Christians in this land. And we'll be sure to have another hilarious adventure with Steve Storyberg along the way!

Story:

There are no empty seats today at the Plaza de Toros de Las Ventas in Madrid, Spain.

In this magnificent arena, all 25,000 seats are filled with people, but most of them are not happy. Yes, the sun is shining. Yes, the skies are blue. Yes, the famous matador, Rodrigo José España is standing in the very middle of the enormous circular playing field, dressed in his blue and gold costume and holding his bright red cape. And yes, the world's most famous bull, Tornado, is about to be released. But there is a problem.

His name is Steve Storyberg.

The security guards are running toward the man with the microphone, as he approaches the matador. They are shouting and waving their hands. Why?

Because Tornado has just been released, and the giant bull is racing at full speed, headed for our brave and bumbling reporter, Steve Storyberg, who has no idea that two very large and very sharp horns are coming up behind him.

"Señor! Get off the field! Señor!" The guards shout, frantically.

"Hello!" Steve calls out. "Señor España, might I have a word with you?"

The matador's eyes are wide. "No. NO!" he shouts.

"Please, sir, just a few questions," Steve asks as he gets closer. "What's it like fighting bulls? And, did you ever get poked by the sharp horns? That would be a problem, I'm sure!"

Suddenly, the muscular security guards tackle Steve and the three of them go tumbling across the field, out of the path of Tornado.

The raging bull rushes the matador, plowing into the red cape which snaps to the side and allows Tornado to pass through, kicking up dirt and dust as he screeches to a stop and turns around.

The crowd cheers wildly, and España bows, then straightens up, ready for Tornado's next move.

In the arena's security room, Steve Storyberg wakes up slowly, pressing the ice pack against his head. Producer Kathleen Connery is facing the camera, going LIVE with the broadcast.

"We're coming to you LIVE from the main security room of the Plaza de Toros de Las Ventas in Madrid. Steve?"

Steve jumps up and faces the camera.

"Hello, I'm Steve Storyberg, and this is Superkid Academy Worldwide News, coming to you super LIVE from the super country of Spain."

Kathleen and cameraman George Lupas and soundman Harrison Borg look at each other and breathe a sigh of relief, all at the same time.

"Spain has so many fascinating things to see…. There is the Museo del Prad in Madrid, one of the world's premier art museums and the exciting running of the bulls in the streets of Pamplona, one of the most famous festivals in Spain. Don't forget the magnificent, unfinished cathedral in Barcelona called the Sagrada Familia and Spain's capital city, Madrid, home to more than 3 million people!"

Steve stops abruptly, as Kathleen whispers to him loudly, pointing at his head. "Ice pack," she says urgently, "ice pack!"

"Eyes back?" Steve says into the microphone.

"ICE PACK!" the entire crew yells.

"No thanks, I've already got one." Steve nods to them as a thank you, and the ice pack slides down his face and falls to the floor. Steve quickly brushes the water from his eyes, then sneezes and smiles.

Kathleen slaps her forehead with her hand. Steve continues.

"Spain has castles, rivers, cities with futuristic buildings, white-sand beaches and towering rock formations. Spain is also home to many kinds of animals: badger, bear, fox and bat. Mongoose, deer and ibex. And…children staring at me!"

Kathleen looks over to see a boy and girl standing next to Steve. She glances at George and Harrison who shrug their shoulders as if to say, "I don't know who they are, either."

Thinking fast, Steve looks down at the boy and girl. "Who are the people of Spain? What do they look like? What do they do? We'll return with those answers and more, right after this."

Kathleen gives the all-clear signal as a string of commercials plays for the viewers, giving Steve and the crew a short break.

"Hello, my young friends," Steve says, looking down at the children, and then, "Hello, sir," as a large security guard with a mustache steps up to him, frowning.

"I'm sorry, señor," the guard says with a Spanish accent. "The children wanted to see you. They know you from television. They were concerned about the incident on the field. May I present, Diego and Isabella."

"Mr. Storyberg!" Isabella, a 9-year-old girl with shiny, black hair, looks up and hands Steve a hamburger and french fries. "My family was concerned when you fell on the ground in front of everybody."

"Oh, yes, that," Steve says, blushing. "Well, I was just…"

"And we knew you like American fast food," Diego says. "You are so funny, Steve, but we thought you might need help."

"Help?" Steve asks with a puzzled look.

"Si, señor. Anyone who walks out into the matador's circle, by himself, with the bull right behind him, you know, it's not a good idea."

"Thank you, Diego," Kathleen says, smiling, now standing next to Steve, holding her microphone. Steve takes a big bite out of the hamburger, as Kathleen continues the broadcast.

"Who are the people of Spain? They are people like Diego and Isabella, who see someone in need and want to help. Tell me kids, are you born-again Christians?"

Both children nod, smiling, while Steve gobbles up 20 french fries at once.

"Wonderful," Kathleen says with a wink. "A very small number of born-again Christians live in Spain, only about 1 percent of the population. But, in the last 12 years, more churches are showing up, and more people are hearing the gospel."

Steve swallows and picks up his microphone.

"That's right, Kathleen. But people are not always hearing the gospel from a preacher. Christians are using more unusual ways to introduce others to Christ. Some believers have opened counseling centers, where people can go when they need help. Some have started English summer camps where young people can come and learn our language and at the same time have an opportunity to hear about Jesus through their new friends."[1]

"Like you, Señor Steve!" Diego says, with a big grin.

"Yes, um, thank you, Diego."

"Our parents have a counseling center here in Madrid," Isabella chimes in.

"Excellent," Steve continues. "As people talk about their problems, the counselors often lead them to Jesus, who has ALL the answers we will ever need."

"My friend Sergio went to a summer camp," Diego tells Steve. "That's where he learned that God loves him. But he still has problems sometimes."

"Yes," Steve nods, "problems still do come up, but God helps us to solve them." Forgetting he's LIVE on TV, Steve takes another big bite of burger. Kathleen steps in to wrap up the broadcast.

"And, with so few Christians in the country, we need to pray that many will hear the gospel and come to Jesus."

Steve finishes chewing and rubs his head, feeling the bump from his fall in the arena.

---

1   "Spain," *The Alliance: Living the Call Together,* The Christian and Missionary Alliance, http://www.cmalliance.org/field/spain (7/11/2013).

"Thank you, Kathleen. And thank you, Isabella and Diego. Join us next time, when I have a more normal day! I'm Steve Storyberg, and this is Superkid Academy Worldwide News." Thinking he's finished, Steve takes another big bite.

While the camera is still running, Isabella hands the ice pack to Steve, who plops it on top of his head.

"I believe I receive my healing!" Steve tries to say, but with his mouth full, it comes out, "Ma meelieve ma meeceeve ma meealing."

Out in the arena, the crowd cheers, the bull snorts, and it's another beautiful day in Spain!

Discussion Questions:

1. **What are some of the unique things about Spain that were mentioned in this story?**

2. **What words can you say in Spanish?**

3. **What loving things did Diego and Isabella do for Steve?**

4. **What creative ways do people use in Spain to reach others for Christ?**

5. **How can you pray specifically for Christians living in Spain?**

Variation No. 1: Ministry Outreaches

Encourage your children to research outreaches in Spain. Choose one that appeals to them and give an offering.

Variation No. 2: Map Skills

Print a blank map of Spain from the Internet. Have your children mark the capital (Madrid), other large cities, major rivers, bordering countries and neighboring bodies of water. Have your children trace this map several times throughout the week to help them remember and gain a better understanding of Spain.

Variation No. 3: Spanish Food

Plan a special Spanish meal for the week with your children. Develop a menu by searching for "traditional Spanish recipes" online and enjoy planning, shopping for and preparing the meal together as a family. Perhaps allow each child to choose one dish (appetizer, main course, side dish, dessert) that they will be responsible to make.

Notes:_____

_____

_____

_____

_____

_____

DAY 3: GIVING LESSON | **A DIFFERENT KIND OF TREASURE**

 Suggested Time: *10 minutes*

 Offering Scripture: Don't store up treasures here on earth, where moths eat them and rust destroys them, and where thieves break in and steal. Store your treasures in heaven, where moths and rust cannot destroy, and thieves do not break in and steal. —Matthew 6:19-20

Supplies: ■ A treasure map (can be created following the instructions below), ■ A treasure box (with old treasures inside)

(Corresponds with Lesson Outline No. III)

Prior to Lesson:

Create old treasures: Soak costume jewelry in water to make it appear rusty and old. Cut small holes in old, dirty clothing to look like moth holes. Include an old, empty wallet or purse with fake coins lying around the bottom of the box. An old treasure map can be created by soaking a heavy piece of parchment paper in tea for a few minutes. Place the treasure box in a hidden area of your home and use the treasure map to locate the box. Allow your children to assist with reading the map and locating the treasure box. Once the treasure box is found, have fun exploring the treasures inside.

Lesson Instructions:

This is a very exciting lesson because we are going on a treasure hunt! Do you enjoy searching for hidden treasures? Great! Let's look over this old treasure map and find the hidden treasure! *(After discovering the hidden treasure box, have fun pulling out the old treasures you'll find inside. Allow time to share about each treasure and allow your children to use their imaginations with the items.)*

Finding this treasure and exploring the contents of the treasure box reminds me of our offering scripture found in Matthew 6:19-20. Let's read it together. "Don't store up treasures here on earth, where moths eat them and rust destroys them, and where thieves break in and steal. Store your treasures in heaven, where moths and rust cannot destroy, and thieves do not break in and steal."

So, what kind of treasures do you think Jesus was talking about in this scripture? *(Allow time for your children to share and discuss their ideas.)* This treasure is just like the one Jesus talked about in our offering scripture. He said we shouldn't store up treasures on earth because they can get rusty, worn out or even stolen. Instead, we should have treasures in heaven. Was Jesus telling us to send our treasures in a big box to heaven? Does the postal service deliver things to heaven? No, Jesus is teaching us to not be so worried about stuff on earth, but instead to look for treasures that will last. What kind of treasure is that? It's people! People are treasures that will last!

When we tell others about Jesus and His goodness, they'll want to ask Him into their hearts. Then they will become a treasure that will be in heaven forever.

Another kind of treasure we can share with others is the fruit of the spirit stored up in the treasure chest of our hearts. We have love, joy, peace, patience and the special fruit of kindness that are better than any gold, silver or jewels. So, as you prepare your offering for this week's church service, remember there is something you can give. You can give someone the blessing of the treasures in your life—Jesus and the fruit of the spirit He has put into your heart. And, those are certainly worth more than old, rusty jewelry or an empty wallet. Those are forever treasures!

Notes:

DAY 4: OBJECT LESSON — GOOD STEERING

 Suggested Time: 10 minutes

 Key Scripture: *Here's my concern: that you care for God's flock with all the diligence of a shepherd.... Not bossily telling others what to do, but tenderly showing them the way.* –1 Peter 5:2-3 MSG

Supplies: ☐ A bridle and a rope (Consider using a rope for both scenarios if a bridle is not available.)

(Corresponds with Lesson Outline No. III)

Lesson Instructions:

Have you ever ridden a horse? I've brought a few important supplies that help when riding a horse. Can anyone tell me what these are and what they're used for? *(Hold the bridle and rope for your children to view. Allow time for discussion.)* Correct! The first item is a bridle. A bridle has a bit that fits into the horse's mouth and is used to steer the horse when riding. The bit attached to the bridle allows the rider to choose which way to go instead of letting the horse decide!

The second piece of equipment is a rope. Sometimes a rope is used to lead a horse by tying it around its neck. Using a rope doesn't usually work as well as using a bridle with a bit. Let's see how this horse equipment ties in to our verse found in 1 Peter 5:2-3 MSG; it says, "Here's my concern: that you care for God's flock with all the diligence of a shepherd.... Not bossily telling others what to do, but tenderly showing them the way."

Do you like it when someone is real bossy, and tells you what to do? They don't ever ask or suggest things, they just try to boss you around. Does that person make you want to do everything they say? Do you feel happy when they give you orders? Well, there are some leaders who treat other people a little bit like the horses we're talking about. They try to force their friends to do what they want, always pushing to get their own way. They don't exercise the fruit of kindness with others. When they do that, it's like the person who ties a rope around the horse's neck and tries to drag it along. But then, there are good leaders who are like the riders who use a bridle. They have a way of gently steering and leading people in the right direction and being patient and kind.

God created each of us to be leaders. We may be leaders on a baseball team, in a dance class, at school or with younger brothers and sisters. We have the fruit of kindness in our hearts, and when we choose to, we can lead others God's way—not by being bossy!

Notes:_____

_____

_____

_____

_____

DAY 5: GAME TIME

PING-PONG GONE WRONG

Suggested Time: 10 minutes

Memory Verse: I, too, try to please everyone in everything I do. I don't just do what is best for me; I do what is best for others so that many may be saved. —1 Corinthians 10:33

Supplies: ■ 2 Aprons, ■ 2 Packets of ping-pong balls, ■ Masking tape, ■ Upbeat music to play during the game (optional)

(Corresponds with Lesson Outline No. III)

Prior to Game:

Choose 2 teams of 2 players each. Create a throw line and a catch line with the masking tape. Fill the buckets with ping-pong balls. 1 player on each team will put on an apron while his/her teammate holds the bucket of ping-pong balls.

Game Instructions:

Players with buckets will throw ping-pong balls to their teammate wearing the apron.

Game Goal:

Whoever catches the most ping-pong balls in his/her apron, without using hands, wins.

Final Word:

A gentle throw is easier to catch than a hard throw. Gentleness is a fruit of the spirit, like kindness, and knowing how and when to be gentle and kind is being just like Jesus.

Notes:_____

_____

_____

_____

_____

_____

_____

ACTIVITY PAGE

GOOD-ATTITUDE WORD SEARCH

 Memory Verse: I, too, try to please everyone in everything I do. I don't just do what is best for me, I do what is best for others so that many may be saved. –1 Corinthians 10:33

(Corresponds with Lesson Outline No. I, III)

This week, you learned that having a good attitude means having a Christ-like attitude. In other words, you should live, act, think and speak like Jesus. Just as He considered others first and gave His life for us, we should live with the same humility and love. In this word search, find 10 words from this week's Bible lesson passage in Philippians 2:1-11.

ATTITUDE	COMPASSIONATE	HONOR
HUMBLE	INTEREST	LOVE
MIND	OBEDIENCE	PURPOSE
TENDER		

```
E V H L X Q H H D Z J E V I H
K T K E C T R T S C D D T Y P
L Q A C H H I L S U S G E F C
R F Z N F M Q L T R W P N Q D
G Z U E O A H I D L E Y D J Y
T B R I F I T I N T E R E S T
N E K D P T S Z I K F V R H P
K D A E A U Y S M U W O O R V
L C L B L T R Q A S N F N L M
Z R R O O H O P X P N W N W O
C S Q E U R C L O I M V B T A
X J A M P G J H M S W O A F E
P T B L J P E A M Z E C C F I
Q L A L B H M R O N O H R L E
E F W E I V S R V M S C P G J
```

ANSWER KEY:

```
E V H L X Q H H D Z J E V I H
K T K E C T R T S C D D T Y P
L Q A C H H I L S U S G E F C
R F Z N F M Q L T R W P N Q D
G Z U E O A H I D L E Y D J Y
T B R I F I T I N T E R E S T
N E K D P T S Z I K F V R H P
K D A E A U Y S M U W O O R V
L C L B L T R Q A S N F N L M
Z R R O O H O P X P N W N W O
C S Q E U R C L O I M V B T A
X J A M P G J H M S W O A F E
P T B L J P E A M Z E C C F I
Q L A L B H M R O N O H R L E
E F W E I V S R V M S C P G J
```

Notes:_____

_____

_____

_____

_____

_____

_____

_____

_____

_____

WEEK 8: GOODNESS

 Memory Verse: And you know that God anointed Jesus of Nazareth with the Holy Spirit and with power. Then Jesus went around doing good and healing all who were oppressed by the devil, for God was with him. —Acts 10:38

WEEK 8: SNAPSHOT — GOODNESS

DAY	TYPE OF LESSON	LESSON TITLE	SUPPLIES
Day 1	Bible Lesson	Tabitha's Goodness	None
Day 2	Real Deal	Milton Hershey	Hershey's® chocolate bars or Hershey's® miniature bars (one per child), Pictures (download to computer screen or print) of Milton Hershey, Hershey factory, the town of Hershey, Hershey School and Hershey Amusement Park
Day 3	Giving Lesson	Lunch Anyone?	1 Individual-sized cooler, 1 Loaf of bread, 1 Packet of tuna that can be torn open
Day 4	Object Lesson	Every Opportunity	Chocolate chip cookies for each child, 1 Glass of milk
Day 5	Game Time	Licorice Launch	14 Licorice super ropes (or enough for each child), 4 Colored buckets, 1 Disposable plastic tarp, Upbeat music (optional)
Bonus	Activity Page	Tabitha's Room-to-Room	1 Copy for each child

Lesson Introduction:

The natural, human inclination is toward selfishness, not generosity. That is why goodness is such a powerful force when it rises up inside us as a supernatural urge to give.

I would be sure to clarify again the difference between goodness and kindness. Kindness is selflessly serving people, even when it's inconvenient. Goodness is meeting their needs by giving them your goods.

Encourage the kids to never be afraid to obey God when He asks them to give. When He asks them to give something away, He always has plans to give back something better! I agree with the saying, "You can't out-give God!"

Love,

Commander Kellie

Commander Kellie

Lesson Outline:

This week, your children will learn about the fruit of goodness. They will discover how satisfying it is to give to others and how much such actions bless God. Help them put this lesson into practice by gathering canned foods for a local food pantry, giving toys and clothes to children in need or collecting coats for a shelter in your area. Explain that giving like this is one more way they can share God's love with a hurting world.

I. DOING GOOD WAS A HABIT WITH JESUS Acts 10:38

a. The force of goodness brings us the godly desire to give of our goods.

b. Goods can be money, food, clothing or toys—anything we own.

c. Jesus went around doing good: healing, preaching and giving to the poor.

d. He had a reputation for it. John 13:29

II. GOODNESS IS PROOF OF GOD IN US

a. When we are selfish, the love of God is not in us. 1 John 3:18

b. Choosing to be a giver is proof that we are God's children—because He's the greatest giver of all time! 3 John 11

c. When we meet a need, we cause people to remember to be thankful to God. 2 Corinthians 9:12

III. IF YOU PLANT GOODNESS, YOU'LL HARVEST GOODNESS

a. Tabitha was known for helping others and giving to the poor. Acts 9:36-41

b. When she became sick and died, Peter prayed for her and she was healed. What a great harvest!

c. You always harvest what you plant, so never quit doing good! Galatians 6:7-10

d. God enables us to be generous with the fruit of goodness. 2 Corinthians 9:8

Notes:_____

_____

_____

_____

_____

_____

_____

_____

DAY 1: BIBLE LESSON — TABITHA'S GOODNESS

 Memory Verse: And you know that God anointed Jesus of Nazareth with the Holy Spirit and with power. Then Jesus went around doing good and healing all who were oppressed by the devil, for God was with him. —Acts 10:38

(Corresponds with Lesson Outline No. I-III)

Today you will study about a woman who exemplified goodness. She was known for her generosity. In fact, when she died, the people she served were so distraught they sought out Peter to heal her. Her generosity encouraged that kind of loyalty, love and friendship. What a testimony of her giving life!

Read Acts 9:36-42:

There was a believer in Joppa named Tabitha (which in Greek is Dorcas). She was always doing kind things for others and helping the poor. About this time she became ill and died. Her body was washed for burial and laid in an upstairs room. But the believers had heard that Peter was nearby at Lydda, so they sent two men to beg him, "Please come as soon as possible!"

So Peter returned with them; and as soon as he arrived, they took him to the upstairs room. The room was filled with widows who were weeping and showing him the coats and other clothes Dorcas had made for them. But Peter asked them all to leave the room; then he knelt and prayed. Turning to the body he said, "Get up, Tabitha." And she opened her eyes! When she saw Peter, she sat up! He gave her his hand and helped her up. Then he called in the widows and all the believers, and he presented her to them alive.

The news spread through the whole town, and many believed in the Lord.

Discussion Questions:

1. **What happened in this story?**

   Allow time for answers.

2. **Why was Tabitha so special to the people?**

   She was known for her goodness. She gave selflessly to the poor.

3. **Who was in the room with her when Peter arrived?**

   There were several widows, for whom she had made coats and clothes.

4. **Why do you think Tabitha (or Dorcas) gave to the widows? What was so special about them?**

   At this time in history, widows were often very poor, because they didn't have husbands to provide for them.

5. How did Tabitha's goodness save her life?

She was dead, but the people she had served called Peter to help. If she had not been such a special and giving person, no one would have cared so much when she died. Her friends loved her enough to want Peter to pray for her.

Variation: Clothes Collection

Use this opportunity to collect clothes or other items for the poor. You can collect from your own home as well as neighbors and extended family. If your children are old enough, allow them to spearhead this effort.

Notes:_____

_____

_____

_____

_____

_____

_____

_____

_____

_____

_____

_____

_____

_____

_____

_____

_____

_____

_____

_____

_____

_____

_____

DAY 2: REAL DEAL | MILTON HERSHEY

 Memory Verse: And you know that God anointed Jesus of Nazareth with the Holy Spirit and with power. Then Jesus went around doing good and healing all who were oppressed by the devil, for God was with him. –Acts 10:38

 Concept: Highlighting an interesting historical place, figure or event that illustrates the theme of the day. The theme of the day is goodness.

 Media: If you have the technical capability, show media photos of Milton Hershey. If you do not have this capability, you may print out photos from the Internet to show the kids or check out a book from your local library.

Supplies: ■ Hershey's® chocolate bars or Hershey's® miniature bars (one per child), ■ Pictures (download to computer screen or print from online source) of Milton Hershey, the Hershey factory, the town of Hershey, Hershey School and Hershey Amusement Park

(Corresponds with Lesson Outline No. I-III)

Intro:

Today, we are learning about goodness. Jesus is the ultimate example of goodness. He shared His goodness by healing those who were sick, giving to those in need and being a friend to all. The man we'll be sharing about today, chose to use the gift of goodness in his life, too. We'll give everyone a hint. *(Unwrap a Hershey's bar and take a bite.)* Mmmmm. Delicious!

Any guesses who we're talking about today?

Lesson Instructions:

What's a philanthropist?

Milton Hershey was a philanthropist.

Does anyone know what a philanthropist is?

A philanthropist is someone who gives their money, goods and services to bless other people without expecting a reward. In Greek, the root word for *philanthropist* means "to love people." When most people think of "Hershey," they think of chocolate. But Milton Hershey did more than make chocolate for America. He was a BIG giver!

About Milton Hershey:

Milton was born in 1857 on a farm in Pennsylvania. He had to quit school in the fourth grade because his family moved around quite a bit.

When Milton landed his first job, he worked as an apprentice for a printer, but disliked it so much that he decided to quit. After that experience, Milton discovered his true love: candy!

Milton became an apprentice for four years for a candy maker, and loved the experience so much, he decided to start his own candy business.

1-2-3 Strikes, You're...Not Out?

Milton borrowed money from his family to start his first candy company in Pennsylvania. The company failed after six years. (Strike one!)

Milton tried again, but this time in Chicago. This company also failed. (Strike two!)

Surely, the third time would be a success! He started a new company, this time in New York City. Again, his company failed. (Strike three!)

Most people would have given up by now, but not Milton! He decided to head back to his hometown in Pennsylvania, where people knew him, and try again. It was a great decision, because Milton's fourth try at the candy business was a home run!

For the next 20 years, Milton's Lancaster Caramel Company was extremely successful. And, that's where the real story begins....

Hershey Chocolate Factory:

Hershey made a lot of money with the success of his caramel factory, so he bought 40,000 acres of land. (That's over 30,000 football fields put together!)

This land wasn't going to be used to make caramel. Milton wanted to make chocolate. And that's the reason he chose to place this factory in the middle of a dairy-farm area. The location would allow Milton to use fresh milk to make real milk chocolate, which at the time was only made in Switzerland.

Hershey had big dreams. He wanted to own the first American company to sell a product to the entire nation. To help this dream come alive, Milton bought chocolate machines from Germany that could produce enough chocolate products to be enjoyed everywhere.

So, in 1905, after two years of building, the Hershey factory was completed. Milton's 5-cent Hershey's® bars were so famous they were called, "The Great American Chocolate Bars."

The Town of Hershey:

Milton decided to build and create an entire town and call it Hershey, Pennsylvania. He built this town specifically for the people who worked for him at the chocolate factory. His goal was to build and create a great place for his workers and their families to have nice homes to live in, send their children to school, enjoy a nice community and have plenty of recreational opportunities. Hershey Park and Hershey Hotel are still open today, if you're interested in a fun road trip! Milton Hershey chose to care for and place value on the needs of his workers and their families, more than spending it all on himself and having lots of "things."

Making History:

One of the biggest joys Milton and his wife, Kitty, had was giving to others. So with money earned from the Hershey Chocolate Company, they chose to bless the lives of many, many people.

In fact, the "seeds of goodness" sown by the Hershey family continue to bless people today, over 100 years later! Now, that's a good harvest! Listed below are "seeds of goodness" sown by the Hershey family:

Hershey School for Orphaned Boys:

Milton and his wife cared about kids and wanted to give them an opportunity to succeed in life. "Unable to have children of their own, Milton and Catherine Hershey decided to use their wealth to create a home and a school for orphaned boys. On November 15, 1909, together they signed the Deed of Trust, extablishing the Hershey Industrial School (renamed Milton Hershey School in 1951). The following year, the first four boys were enrolled and began to live and attend classes in The Homestead, the birthplace of Milton Hershey, which he had purchased a few years before."[1]

In 1945, as Milton was approaching the end of his life, he transferred his remaining assets to the trust to make sure the school would continue. Today, the Milton Hershey School (MHS) is still a residential facility that now serves more than 1800 pre-K-12th grade boys and girls of all races who are in financial and social need, providing education, housing, food, medical and psychological health care, recreational opportunities and clothing at no cost to the families.[2]

Penn State Hershey Medical Center:

Founded in 1963 through a $50 million grant from The Milton S. Hershey Foundation, 18 years after the death of Milton Hershey, this research and teaching hospital, part of Pennsylvania State University, also houses a children's hospital—further continuing Milton and Kitty's dream of helping children.[3]

A top-notch hospital, more than 170 Penn State Hershey Medical doctors were named to the Best Doctors in America® 2013 list.[4]

Adding a Little "Sweetness" to World War II:

During World War II, Hershey wanted to brighten each soldier's day with a little "sweetness." So during the entire war, Milton supplied the U.S. military with chocolate bars. The emergency field ration "Tropical Bar" was created specifically for the soldiers because it would not melt in tropical weather. Hershey Field Ration D chocolate bars become so successful that they became a standard part of a soldier's "C Rations" during World War II. [5]

By the end of the war, Hershey was sending 24 million bars of chocolate a week to the soldiers! For this

1   "Milton Hershey School: Story Behind the School," http//www.mhs-pa.org/history/story-behind-the-school (5/1/2013).

2   Milton Hershey School, http://www.mhs-pa.org/about/frequently-asked-questions (5/1/2013).

3   PennState Hershey, http://www.pennstatehershey.org/web/guest/home (5/1/13).

4   PennState Hershey..

5   "Price of Freedom: Americans at War," http://amhistory.si.edu/militaryhistory/collection/object.asp?ID=42 (5/1/2013).

outstanding gift, on August 22, 1942, the Hershey Chocolate Corporation received five Army-Navy "E" Production Awards for their war effort. The corporation was awarded with a special flag to fly over the chocolate plant and a lapel pin for every worker.[6]

Outro:

So, the next time you enjoy a Hershey's chocolate bar, remember all the "seeds of goodness" sown and harvested by Milton and Kitty Hershey. Milton Hershey knew chocolate only lasts a moment, but acts of goodness will be remembered forever. God knows our hearts and remembers what we do for others! That's why Milton Hershey is today's Real Deal.

Variation: Teen Helper

If you have a teenage child, recruit them to dress up as Milton Hershey. The costume could include a white button-up shirt, dark suit, bow tie and neatly combed hair.

Notes:

---

6   "Price of Freedom: Americans at War."

DAY 3: GIVING LESSON | **LUNCH ANYONE?**

 Suggested Time: 10 minutes

 Offering Scripture: One of the disciples—it was Andrew, brother to Simon Peter—said, "There's a little boy here who has five barley loaves and two fish. But that's a drop in the bucket for a crowd like this." —John 6:8-9 MSG

Supplies: ☐ 1 Individual-sized cooler, ☐ 1 Loaf of bread, ☐ 1 Packet of tuna that can be torn open

(Corresponds with Lesson Outline No. I-III)

Lesson Instructions:

Wow, I am so hungry! In fact, I have a little snack. I have my favorite bread here *(smell it)*. Mmmm, that smells great. And I also brought some tuna fish. *(Open the tuna so the smell can help set the stage of your story.)* Yummy, bread and fish! Come to think of it, this snack makes me think of a story I read in John. It's cool because it's about a kid, just like one of you. Let me read it to you. *(Read John 6:5-13 MSG.)*

How amazing is that? God used just one boy's lunch to feed thousands of people, with plenty of leftovers, too—12 baskets full to be exact. But I was thinking, *What if that boy had not given his lunch to Jesus? What if he had started thinking, I'm too hungry, I need to eat this lunch myself?* That kid didn't know Jesus was going to feed the whole crowd with his lunch. He may have just thought that Jesus was hungry, so he brought Him something to eat! Think about it—there was a huge group of people who had something good to eat because a little boy decided to be a giver and brought what he had to Jesus.

Superkids, be ready to share what you have! The next time you feel that little tug in your heart to do something generous, be like the boy with the fish. Don't hold back. Step right up and give what you have. You do that, and the Lord will be right there to make your little into a lot!

Variation: Fish and Loaves

If tuna fish is not a good choice for your family, substitute fish sticks. You could even create small baskets of fish sticks and bread loaves for each child or family member.

Notes:_____

_____

_____

_____

_____

DAY 4: OBJECT LESSON   **EVERY OPPORTUNITY**

Suggested Time: 5-8 minutes

Key Scripture: *Whenever we have the opportunity, we should do good to everyone....* –Galatians 6:10

Supplies: ☐ *Chocolate chip cookies for each child,* ☐ *1 Glass of milk*

(Corresponds with Lesson Outline No. I-III)

Lesson Instructions:

Chocolate chip cookies are great—especially with a big glass of milk! *(Take a bite of the cookie and a sip of the milk as the lesson continues.)* This is one, good cookie, so soft and chewy. Mmmmm, great stuff! Oh, I almost forgot why I was here. I wanted to share a verse with you. It's Galatians 6:10, which says, "Whenever we have the opportunity, we should do good to everyone...." That's a great verse. That means that every chance we get, we should be good to the people around us. I definitely do that! Whenever I get a chance, I try to be good to others—even if it means sharing my stuff. *(Keep talking about how you obey that verse until your children start responding that you aren't sharing your cookies.)*

Oh! You mean you like homemade chocolate chip cookies, too? Wow, you do? I could share a few, but I'm not really in a sharing mood. Sometimes you just don't feel like sharing, you know! *(Take another bite of the cookie.)* Mmmmm, this is so good, and I'm pretty hungry, too. *(Continue to act preoccupied with eating the cookie, ignoring the children and playing up how good it is.)*

(As if it slowly dawns on you...) You know, I guess by eating this cookie all by myself, I'm not being very good to those around me, am I, because I'm not sharing my cookies. I guess I wasn't taking every opportunity to do good to those around me. That includes sharing the good things I have with others, doesn't it? Well, this has been a good reminder, and I'm changing that right now!

We want to be like Jesus and do good whenever we have the chance. And we have a chance today with these cookies.

Sooo, who would like a chocolate chip cookie? *(Pass the rest of the cookies to your children.)* That's actually more fun than eating the cookies by myself. I'm going to share goodness more often. In fact, I'm going to do just like Galatians 6:10 says and do good every opportunity I get!

Notes:_____

_____

_____

_____

_____

DAY 5: GAME TIME — LICORICE LAUNCH

 Suggested Time: 10 minutes

 Memory Verse: And you know that God anointed Jesus of Nazareth with the Holy Spirit and with power. Then Jesus went around doing good and healing all who were oppressed by the devil, for God was with him. —Acts 10:38

Supplies: ☐ 14 Licorice super ropes (or enough for each child), ☐ 4 Colored buckets, ☐ 1 Disposable plastic tarp, ☐ Upbeat music to play during the game (optional)

(Corresponds with Lesson Outline No. I-II)

Prior to Game:

Create a "launch line" with masking tape, cones or a licorice rope. Spread the tarp over the "landing" area. This game can be played indoors or outdoors. Place buckets in various locations on the "landing" area, for each contestant.

Game Instructions:

Choose 4 players to line up side by side at the "launch line," each holding a licorice rope. Contestants will face the "landing" area. Each contestant will have a bucket as his/her target. When music begins, each contestant will bite off a piece of licorice and "launch" it into his/her respective bucket. Each time a piece of licorice lands in a bucket, have spectators shout, "Oh my goodness!"

Game Goal:

The player with the most pieces of licorice in his/her bucket, wins. Reward winners with their own licorice rope to enjoy!

Final Word:

"Wow, you really made that licorice go a long way! Goodness is like that. It can go further than we think it will. Licorice can be really good, but God's goodness, working through us, is even better and longer lasting than a licorice rope!" Remind your Superkids that if Jesus went around doing good, we should go around doing good every chance we get!

Variation: Smaller Groups

This game can be played with fewer players. Simply adjust the number of licorice ropes and buckets. Or, if materials or space is a concern, play several rounds.

Notes:_____

_____

_____

_____

_____

_____

_____

_____

_____

_____

_____

_____

_____

_____

_____

_____

_____

_____

_____

_____

_____

_____

_____

_____

_____

_____

_____

_____

_____

_____

_____

ACTIVITY PAGE

TABITHA'S ROOM-TO-ROOM

Memory Verse: And you know that God anointed Jesus of Nazareth with the Holy Spirit and with power. Then Jesus went around doing good and healing all who were oppressed by the devil, for God was with him. —Acts 10:38

(Corresponds with Lesson Outline No. I-II)

In this week's Bible lesson, you learned about a woman named Tabitha. She lived a generous life, making and giving clothes to the poor. Now, compare the two pictures of the room where she was healed. Find 10 differences between the two pictures.

WEEK 9: FAITH

 Memory Verse: Faith is the confidence that what we hope for will actually happen; it gives us assurance about things we cannot see. —Hebrews 11:1

WEEK 9: SNAPSHOT

FAITH

DAY	TYPE OF LESSON	LESSON TITLE	SUPPLIES
Day 1	Bible Lesson	Leaders of Faith	None
Day 2	Read-Aloud	Superkid Academy Worldwide: England	Images of England—historic castles and homes, Buckingham Palace, the Queen's Guard (palace guards),Tower of London, beautiful countryside, people, London bobbies, Roman ruins, cities (London, Birmingham, Canterbury, Bristol, etc.)
Day 3	Giving Lesson	Make It Happen	Milk, Chocolate syrup, Drinking glasses (1 per child), Spoons
Day 4	Academy Lab	"Eye" Spy Someone Faithful	Card stock, Tape, Modeling clay, Tissue paper, Magnifying glass, Scissors, Flashlight, Round goldfish bowl (filled with water)
Day 5	Game Time	Javelin Toss	Cones or masking tape, 2 Pool noodles, 2 Hula Hoops®, 2 Hula-Hoop® stands, Stopwatch (or watch with a second hand) Optional: Upbeat music
Bonus	Activity Page	Leaders of Faith Match	1 Copy for each child

Lesson Introduction:

Because God's nature has been born inside us, we have His faith and His faithfulness to use. This is a powerful living principle that your Superkids will benefit from understanding for the rest of their lives!

God's faith(fulness) inside us helps us choose to walk in the fruit of the spirit when our flesh wants to do something else. We walk in love when we want to be rude, joy when we'd rather cry, peace instead of worry, patience when we want to give up. We are kind when we want to be selfish. We walk in goodness not stinginess, we are full of faith when circumstances look bad. Gentleness comes out when we want to fight, and self-control kicks in when our flesh is screaming, "Let me be in charge!" We can absolutely win in every instance.

God wants us to be extraordinary superheroes, too! He has given us superpowers to do it with. Remember, the Father takes no pleasure in those who turn away, so tell your children to be found faithful.

Love,

Commander Kellie

Commander Kellie

Lesson Outline:

Faithfulness is a vital part of living the successful Christian life. Throughout the Old Testament, men and women accomplished great things for God because of their commitment to His promises. And, how much more can we accomplish for Him now that we have the Holy Spirit at work in us! This week, enjoy learning about these men and women of faith. Discover how God used them and continues to use faithful people to do His will.

I. THE HEROES OF FAITH DIDN'T LOOK AT CIRCUMSTANCES
Hebrews 11

a. Noah built a boat before rain or floods even existed. (Verse 7)

b. Abraham believed God would raise Isaac from the dead. (Verse 17)

c. Moses served God instead of Pharaoh. Moses expected God to make a way through the Red Sea, even though it looked BAD! (Verses 24-25, 27)

d. They were great heroes, but they didn't have what we have! (Verse 39)

II. WHAT WAS THE GREAT THING GOD HAD IN MIND?
Hebrews 11:40

a. That His own nature (God's DNA) would dwell in us—more heroes of faith!

- God is not done making heroes out of ordinary, everyday kids!

- He's still looking for someone who believes Him.

- Will He find a Superkid today who can be one of God's heroes of faith?

b. We have God's very own faith and faithfulness to use!

c. Faith helps us live by what God says and not by what we see. 2 Corinthians 5:7

d. Take the faith test. Is your faith in Jesus visible? 2 Corinthians 13:5

"Examine yourselves to see if your faith is genuine. Test yourselves."

III. HIS FAITHFULNESS HELPS US CHOOSE FRUIT WHEN WE NEED IT

a. Faithfulness helps us be faithful and full of faith too! 1 Corinthians 4:2

b. We can choose to trust His Word, and do things His way.

c. Will He find faith when He returns? YES! Luke 18:8

Notes:_____

_____

_____

DAY 1: BIBLE LESSON   **LEADERS OF FAITH**

 Memory Verse: Faith is the confidence that what we hope for will actually happen; it gives us assurance about things we cannot see. –Hebrews 11:1

(Corresponds with Lesson Outline No. I-III)

Today, we're studying about great examples of faith in scripture. Feel free to delve deeper into any of these examples with your children by going to the original passages in the Old Testament. This is a great chance to teach your children about their spiritual heritage and the mighty God they serve!

Read Hebrews 11:1-40:
Great Examples of Faith

Faith is the confidence that what we hope for will actually happen; it gives us assurance about things we cannot see. Through their faith, the people in days of old earned a good reputation.

By faith we understand that the entire universe was formed at God's command, that what we now see did not come from anything that can be seen.

It was by faith that Abel brought a more acceptable offering to God than Cain did. Abel's offering gave evidence that he was a righteous man, and God showed his approval of his gifts. Although Abel is long dead, he still speaks to us by his example of faith.

It was by faith that Enoch was taken up to heaven without dying—"he disappeared, because God took him." For before he was taken up, he was known as a person who pleased God. And it is impossible to please God without faith. Anyone who wants to come to him must believe that God exists and that he rewards those who sincerely seek him.

It was by faith that Noah built a large boat to save his family from the flood. He obeyed God, who warned him about things that had never happened before. By his faith Noah condemned the rest of the world, and he received the righteousness that comes by faith.

It was by faith that Abraham obeyed when God called him to leave home and go to another land that God would give him as his inheritance. He went without knowing where he was going. And even when he reached the land God promised him, he lived there by faith—for he was like a foreigner, living in tents. And so did Isaac and Jacob, who inherited the same promise. Abraham was confidently looking forward to a city with eternal foundations, a city designed and built by God.

It was by faith that even Sarah was able to have a child, though she was barren and was too old. She believed that God would keep his promise. And so a whole nation came from this one man who was as good as dead—a nation with so many people that, like the stars in the sky and the sand on the seashore, there is no way to count them.

All these people died still believing what God had promised them. They did not receive what was promised, but they saw it all from a distance and welcomed it. They agreed that they were foreigners and nomads here on earth. Obviously people who say such things are looking forward to a country they can call their own. If they had longed for the country they came from, they could have gone back. But they were looking for a better place, a heavenly homeland. That is why God is not ashamed to be called their God, for he has prepared a city for them.

It was by faith that Abraham offered Isaac as a sacrifice when God was testing him. Abraham, who had received God's promises, was ready to sacrifice his only son, Isaac, even though God had told him, "Isaac is the son through whom your descendants will be counted." Abraham reasoned that if Isaac died, God was able to bring him back to life again. And in a sense, Abraham did receive his son back from the dead.

It was by faith that Isaac promised blessings for the future to his sons, Jacob and Esau.

It was by faith that Jacob, when he was old and dying, blessed each of Joseph's sons and bowed in worship as he leaned on his staff.

It was by faith that Joseph, when he was about to die, said confidently that the people of Israel would leave Egypt. He even commanded them to take his bones with them when they left.

It was by faith that Moses' parents hid him for three months when he was born. They saw that God had given them an unusual child, and they were not afraid to disobey the king's command.

It was by faith that Moses, when he grew up, refused to be called the son of Pharaoh's daughter. He chose to share the oppression of God's people instead of enjoying the fleeting pleasures of sin. He thought it was better to suffer for the sake of Christ than to own the treasures of Egypt, for he was looking ahead to his great reward. It was by faith that Moses left the land of Egypt, not fearing the king's anger. He kept right on going because he kept his eyes on the one who is invisible. It was by faith that Moses commanded the people of Israel to keep the Passover and to sprinkle blood on the doorposts so that the angel of death would not kill their firstborn sons.

It was by faith that the people of Israel went right through the Red Sea as though they were on dry ground. But when the Egyptians tried to follow, they were all drowned.

It was by faith that the people of Israel marched around Jericho for seven days, and the walls came crashing down.

It was by faith that Rahab the prostitute was not destroyed with the people in her city who refused to obey God. For she had given a friendly welcome to the spies.

How much more do I need to say? It would take too long to recount the stories of the faith of Gideon, Barak, Samson, Jephthah, David, Samuel, and all the prophets. By faith these people overthrew kingdoms, ruled with justice, and received what God had promised them. They shut the mouths of lions, quenched the flames of fire, and escaped death by the edge of the sword. Their weakness was turned to strength. They became strong in battle and put whole armies to flight. Women received their loved ones back again from death.

But others were tortured, refusing to turn from God in order to be set free. They placed their hope in a better life after the resurrection. Some were jeered at, and their backs were cut open with whips. Others were chained in prisons. Some died by stoning, some were sawed in half, and others were killed with the sword. Some went about wearing skins of sheep and goats, destitute and oppressed and mistreated. They were too good for this world, wandering over deserts and mountains, hiding in caves and holes in the ground.

All these people earned a good reputation because of their faith, yet none of them received all that God had promised. For God had something better in mind for us, so that they would not reach perfection without us.

Discussion Questions:

1. **Review the different leaders from the passage. Discuss what they did and why they were listed here.**

2. **What did all the people listed in this passage have in common?**

   They all had great faith.

3. **What does it mean to have faith?**

   Having faith means to trust God and His Word no matter what.

4. **Can you think of a person in your life who has exhibited great faith?**

   Answers will vary.

Variation No. 1: Deeper Bible Study

As your children study these leaders of faith, consider incorporating other tools into your Bible study like a concordance, Bible dictionary, Bible maps and a Greek/Hebrew Bible. Teach your children what each of these tools are, and how and when to use them.

Variation No. 2: Writing Assignment

For older children, consider assigning a writing project that researches one of the leaders listed in this chapter, perhaps one of the leaders listed in verse 32 (ex: Gideon, Barak, Samson, Jephthah, David, Samuel or one of the prophets). Ask your children to explain how the person exhibited great faith, why and what resulted from it. If you have incorporated other study tools (Bible maps, Bible dictionary, etc.), ask them to incorporate these tools in this writing assignment.

Notes:_____

_____

_____

_____

_____

_____

_____

_____

_____

DAY 2: READ-ALOUD | **SUPERKID ACADEMY WORLDWIDE: ENGLAND**

 Suggested Time: 15 minutes

 Key Scripture: For God, who said, "Let there be light in the darkness," has made this light shine in our hearts so we could know the glory of God.... –2 Corinthians 4:6

Supplies: ■ Images of England—historic castles and homes, Buckingham Palace, the Queen's Guard (palace guards), Tower of London, beautiful countryside, people, London bobbies, Roman ruins, cities (London, Birmingham, Canterbury, Bristol, etc.)

Background:

This week, our Superkid Academy Worldwide read-aloud story finds Steve Storyberg and crew under cloudy skies in London, England, in the United Kingdom. Not only will they meet two brilliant detectives, but they'll see a spot of spiritual sunshine that will brighten everybody's day!

Story:

LONDON, ENGLAND. 5:00 a.m.: Steve Storyberg and his camera crew sneak quietly along a cobblestone street, recording a broadcast for the next morning.

Trying his best to move forward in complete silence, Steve suddenly steps on an egg that spurts out goopy egg stuff, which makes him slip backward and slam, clattering, into a trash can. This scares a cat, which triggers the barking of an excited terrier that chases the cat into the darkness, which draws the attention of a local bobby (policeman),[1] who steps over to Steve Storyberg lying flat on his back in the street.

"And what seems to be the problem 'ere?" asks the tall policeman.

"Hello," Steve says, jumping to his feet and continuing the broadcast. "I'm Steve Storyberg, and this is Super-kid Academy Worldwide News, coming to you super LIVE from the super city of London, the capital of England in the United Kingdom, home to more than 8 million people. England is filled with historic castles, the royal palace of Queen Elizabeth, beautiful countryside and wonderful people! You can even find ruins from the Roman occupation here in the first century..."

"'Why, 'ello, Mr. Storyberg!" the policeman exclaims, "I watch your show on the telly! Pleased as punch to meet you, I am, sir. Bit early for you to be out 'ere snoopin' 'round at this hour, eh?"

Steve explains that he's trying to find the two most famous detectives in London, but they're nowhere to be found. "It's a mystery," Steve whispers out loud.

"Not really, sir! That would be the two of 'em right over there. Found their lost dog and cat by the looks of it."

"So they have," Steve says, straightening his tie and tiptoeing over to the two identically dressed detectives, each with a long, black overcoat, plaid deerstalker hat and large magnifying glass in hand.

---

1   "Project Britain: Your Guide to British Life, Culture and Customs," 2011 Mandy Barrow, http://projectbritain.com/london/crime.htm.

Steve and the crew kneel down behind some trash cans and Steve whispers into the mic. "I can see them now. Two detectives: One is Gridlock Jones from Los Angeles, and the other is Smartclock Scones from here in London. Which is which, I wonder…?"

"Cup of coffee, my friend?" one detective asks the other.

"Not for me, sir. Spot o' tea more to my liking," answers the other detective.

"Strange," the first detective replies, "as long as I've been a detective, drivin' on the right side of the road, spendin' dollars and saying 'hi' to folks, I've never met a dude who doesn't drink coffee."

"Not so strange, my man," answers the other detective. "As long as I've been a detective, driving on the *left-hand* side of the road, spending pounds and saying 'cheerio,' I've never met a chap who doesn't enjoy a good cup o' tea!"

"Ahaaa!" shouts Steve, jumping up. "I've solved the mystery. The man drinking tea is none other than Smartclock Scones, and the man sipping coffee is Gridlock Jones! Their accents gave them away!"

"Right you are, sir," remarks Smartclock, "but another mystery remains to be solved. Which of us owns the feline, and which one the canine?"

Steve scratches his head, and closes his eyes, deep in thought. "Could you repeat the question?" he asks.

"No need to repeat the question!" Producer Kathleen Connery announces, stepping in front of Steve, on her own mic. "The solution is already in the cup."

"The cup?" Both detectives say at the same time.

"Huh?" says Steve. "They both have cups. Which one?"

"Elementary, my dear Storyberg," answers Kathleen. "Simply put the coffee cup on the ground and watch what happens."

Gridlock Jones takes a final sip of coffee and places the white cup on the cobblestone street. The cat saunters over and licks the inside, lapping up the remaining milk. This makes the dog hungry. He trots over to his owner, Smartclock, and whines, begging for breakfast.

"Mystery solved," Kathleen says. The camera stops. But as footsteps are heard coming around the corner, Kathleen tells cameraman Harrison Borg to click the camera back on.

The tall bobby rounds the corner, holding the morning newspaper.

"Don't mean to interrupt…couldn't help but notice, looking in the paper, strange things happening 'round 'ere of late in our city—strange things that might somehow be tied together."

"Proceed," commands Scones.

"Go on," requests Jones.

"Tell us more," says Kathleen.

The policeman continues, "It's been 'appening for a while now. Churches here seem to be filling up. More and more people, every Sunday. And not for fish and chips, mind you. People just coming. And there's more noise, too."

"What kind of noise?" probes Scones.

"Loud singing, clapping and even some dancing, eh? Extraordinary! And the little ones comin' 'round, as well. I walked by a big church and heard the little ones laughing and playing in church!"[2]

"Sounds like some great things are happening here in England!" remarks Jones.

"But that's not the strangest thing," the bobby continues. "There's more."

"Speak up, man!" instructs Scones.

"Yes, sir. Last year in London, a big crowd gathered together—over 5,000, the constable told me. (And he's good at counting, he is!)"

"Immaterial! Go on," blurts Scones.

"People were listening to a nice chap from the States speak from the Bible: a Mr. Copeland, I believe. And the next day, his wife did the talking. Sick people were made better—healed, I guess you'd say—right there on the spot. Without a doctor or a nurse!"[3]

The policeman slumps down on a garbage can, his eyes tearing up. "Truth told, I was there. I've not been the same since," he said, turning away to wipe his eyes. "Strangest thing...." Regaining his bobby composure, he looks up at them.

"I have the answer!" Steve Storyberg announces. "It's plain to see that God is touching people's lives. It's the power of God that comes with the presence of God. Like the light that shines when a light bulb is turned on!"

At that very moment, the streetlights turn off, and Steve frowns. But then, with an even brighter light, the sun breaks through the leaden clouds overhead, shining beams of cheerful morning sunshine down on the old cobblestones.

Steve grabs his mic and faces the camera.

"Ladies and gentlemen, you see these beams of light, but a greater light, God's light, is shining today, right here in London. And what a difference it's making! I'm Steve Storyberg, Superkid Academy Worldwide News, coming to you super LIVE from the super city of London, England."

Just then, the famous London clock, Big Ben, chimes, and a friendly chimney sweep, swinging his broom, walks toward them.

"Fancy that!" says the bobby, "I sat next to him at the big meeting last year. Hello, Burt!"

The chimney sweep chuckles and rhymes his answer: "Cleaning the city and cleaning the streets, singin' 'bout God to everyone I meets!"

Harrison swings the camera around to capture the scene, while Kathleen thinks to herself, *Wow! This may be the best show we've ever done!*

---

2   "Ministry With Children," *The Church of England, A Christian Presence in Every Community,* http://www.churchofengland.org/education/children-young-people/ministry-with-children.aspx (7/11/2013).

3   To watch Kenneth Copeland 2012 Europe Victory Campaign or other meetings, go to BVOV.TV/click on "Miss a service or want to watch it again?"/2012 Meetings/2012 Europe Victory Campaign or any other in the listing (7/11/2013).

Discussion Questions:

1. Why would the policeman feel that God's ways of working were "strange"?

2. How would you explain the amazing works of God to the policeman?

3. How would you pray for these new believers in England?

4. How many things can you think of that are unique to living in England, or unique to living in America?

5. What is your favorite part about this story?

Variation No. 1: Reading

Visit your local library to borrow books about England. Read them throughout the week.

Variation No. 2: Writing Assignment

For older children, consider assigning a 1-2 page paper on England and what God is doing there. Have your children include:

- Key information about England

- Significant ministry outreaches happening within England (like KCM Europe) and/or coming out of England to the rest of the world

- Famous Christian leaders from England

- Your child's recommendation for reaching the lost in England.*

*For Kenneth Copeland Ministries outreach information, go to kcm.org.uk.

Variation No. 3: Map Skills

Print a blank map of England from the Internet. Have your children mark the capital (London), other large cities, major rivers, bordering countries and neighboring bodies of water. Have your children trace this map several times throughout the week to help them remember and gain better understanding of England.

DAY 3: GIVING LESSON

MAKE IT HAPPEN

 Suggested Time: *10 minutes*

 Offering Scripture: *...faith without deeds is dead.* –James 2:26 NIV

Supplies: ■ Milk, ■ Chocolate syrup, ■ Drinking glasses (1 per child), ■ Spoons

(Corresponds with Lesson Outline No. I, III)

Lesson Instructions:

Does anyone know what these ingredients can be used to create? Yes, chocolate milk! There seems to be a challenge, though. We have all the necessary ingredients, but how do we turn this into a tasty beverage?

Does one of you know what's needed to make a tasty glass of chocolate milk? *(Let your children walk you through the process of pouring the milk, adding the chocolate and then stirring it all together—three action steps.)* Great job! We had all the necessary ingredients to create chocolate milk, but until we actually combined the ingredients and stirred them together, there wasn't any chocolate milk to drink.

This is similar to what James 2:26 says, "...faith without deeds is dead." We can say that we believe God is faithful to His Word, will answer our prayers and provide what we need, but until we take some action and actually do what the Bible says, our faith will not work. God's Word instructs us to be givers. When we give and bless others, He will bless us in return. Our part is to obey His Word. That's the action part we do, so that our faith can work and God can do His part to bless us!

Today, as we prepare our offerings for service, we are putting action to our faith. It's similar to stirring up the chocolate milk and knowing something good is on the way!

Notes:_____

_____

_____

_____

_____

_____

_____

_____

_____

DAY 4: ACADEMY LAB

"EYE" SPY SOMEONE FAITHFUL

 Suggested Time: 10 minutes

 Key Scripture: For we live by believing and not by seeing. –2 Corinthians 5:7

 Teacher Tip: Preparing this experiment prior to your lesson will help with the flow of the demonstration.

Supplies: ☐ Card stock, ☐ Tape, ☐ Modeling clay, ☐ Tissue paper, ☐ Magnifying glass, ☐ Scissors, ☐ Flashlight, ☐ Round goldfish bowl (filled with water)

(Corresponds with Lesson Outline No. I-III)

Prior to Lesson:

Tape tissue paper to one side of the goldfish bowl.

Place the magnifying glass in front of the bowl, using the molding clay to hold it upright. (The magnifying glass will be located on the side opposite the tissue paper.)

Fold a piece of card stock in half and cut out a shape, the same way you would make a paper doll (ex: a cross, a tree, a heart, etc.).

Place the cutout card in front of the magnifying glass, using the modeling clay to hold it upright, as you did with the magnifying glass. (The magnifying glass will be located in between the goldfish bowl and the card.)

Shine the flashlight on the cutout shape. An upside-down image will appear on the tissue paper. Move the magnifying glass back and forth to make the image sharper.

Dimming the room lights may make the image easier to see.

Lesson Instructions:

Today, we have a very interesting experiment!

Can anyone guess what will happen when we shine the flashlight on this shape?

(Talk about the preparation of the experiment, and allow time for your children to share their ideas.)

It's interesting that when the flashlight shines on each cutout shape, it appears upside down on the paper. This experiment reminds me of the verse found in 2 Corinthians 5:7 that says, "For we live by believing and not by seeing."

The shapes did not appear the same when the flashlight was shining on them through the magnifying glass. If we weren't able to see the original cutout, we might believe that the shape were really upside down.

Sometimes, it's easier to believe what we see instead of what God's Word says.

There are people who only believe what their eyes can see, but we're not like that when we have Jesus in our hearts. God's people live by what they *believe.* The Bible calls this living by faith.

Now, about those people who only believe what their eyes can see—we can help them! In fact, Jesus told one of His closest friends, named Thomas, something really cool. He said, "You believe because you've seen with your own eyes. Even better blessings are in store for those who believe without seeing" (John 20:29 MSG). If we are living our lives the way the Lord has asked us to, then others will be able to SEE Jesus when they look at us. And that kind of seeing will make believers out of them, too!

Notes:

DAY 5: GAME TIME

JAVELIN TOSS

 Suggested Time: 10 minutes

 Memory Verse: Faith is the confidence that what we hope for will actually happen; it gives us assurance about things we cannot see. –Hebrews 11:1

 Teacher Tip: Hula-Hoop® stands can be found at toy stores or online, or can be easily made from foam blocks found at craft stores. Cut a slit through the top of a wide foam block, large enough to tightly wedge the hoop into. This will hold it upright.

 Family Helper: Enlist one family member to move the stands back to the next station once a player has successfully thrown his/her pool noodle through the hoop. Since this is a race, the person must be able to do this quickly.

Supplies: ☐ Cones or masking tape, ☐ 2 Pool noodles, ☐ 2 Hula Hoops®, ☐ 2 Hula-Hoop® stands, ☐ Stopwatch (or watch with a second hand), ☐ Optional: Upbeat music (to play during game)

(Corresponds with Lesson Outline No. I, II g)

Prior to Game:

This game is best played outdoors. Create a "toss line" with cones or masking tape.

Place the hoops in the stands, side by side, 4 feet from the toss line. (Adjust spacing for younger players.)

Behind the hoops, mark 4 additional spots. Initially, place the stand 4 feet from the start line. Behind that spot, place another line 1 foot behind the stand (5 feet from the start line); the next line 1 foot behind that line (6 feet from the start line), and so on. The hoop stands will have a total of 5 locations. These spots can be marked using additional cones or items from around your house.

2 players will compete against each other.

Place pool noodles behind the toss line.

If you have more than 2 players, play multiple rounds until a winner is determined.

Game Instructions:

Let's begin by saying our memory verse together:

Hebrews 11:1 says, "Faith is the confidence that what we hope for will actually happen; it gives us assurance about things we cannot see."

Today's activity is a pool-noodle-tossing contest!

When the game starts, each player will toss his/her pool noodle through the Hula Hoop®. The pool noodle must go through the hoop before we can move the stand back to the next line.

Continue with several rounds, as time permits.

Game Goal:

The first player who successfully throws his/her pool noodle through the hoop at all 5 stations, wins.

Final Word:

Hitting the Hula-Hoop® goals can be difficult, but we can hit our goals when we trust in God and exercise our faith!

Notes:_____

_____

_____

_____

_____

_____

_____

_____

_____

_____

_____

_____

_____

_____

_____

_____

_____

_____

_____

_____

_____

ACTIVITY PAGE

LEADERS OF FAITH MATCH

Memory Verse: Faith is the confidence that what we hope for will actually happen; it gives us assurance about things we cannot see. —Hebrews 11:1

(Corresponds with Lesson Outline No. I)

This week in your Bible Lesson, you read about many leaders of faith in the Old Testament. Match the person with the act that he or she accomplished.

Leader of Faith:

1. Abel
2. Enoch
3. Noah
4. Abraham
5. Sarah
6. Jacob
7. Joseph
8. Joshua
9. Moses' parents
10. Moses
11. The people of Israel
12. Rahab

Act of Faith:

a. Hid him for three months when he was born.

b. Built a large boat to save his family from the flood.

c. Marched around Jericho for seven days, and the walls came crashing down.

d. Was not destroyed with the people in her city who refused to obey God because she had given a friendly welcome to Israel's spies.

e. Blessed each of Joseph's sons and bowed in worship as he leaned on his staff.

f. Offered Isaac as a sacrifice when he was tested.

g. Refused to be called the son of Pharaoh's daughter and instead chose to share the oppression of God's people instead of enjoying the fleeting pleasures of sin.

h. Brought a more acceptable offering to God than Cain did.

i. Was taken up to heaven without dying.

j. Was able to have a child, though she was barren and too old.

k. Said confidently that the people of Israel would leave Egypt.

l. Went right through the Red Sea as though they were on dry ground.

ANSWER KEY:

1. h
2. i
3. b
4. f
5. j
6. e
7. k
8. c
9. a
10. g
11. l
12. d

Notes:_____

_____

_____

_____

_____

_____

_____

_____

_____

_____

_____

_____

_____

_____

_____

_____

_____

_____

WEEK 10: GENTLENESS

 Memory Verse: They must not slander anyone and must avoid quarreling. Instead, they should be gentle and show true humility to everyone. —Titus 3:2

WEEK 10: SNAPSHOT — GENTLENESS

DAY	TYPE OF LESSON	LESSON TITLE	SUPPLIES
Day 1	Bible Lesson	Jesus' Gentleness	None
Day 2	Academy Lab	Take It Easy	1 Egg, 4 Eggshell halves, Scissors, Masking tape, Books
Day 3	Giving Lesson	Laws Are Good!	A police uniform and hat
Day 4	Real Deal	Oskar Schindler	Optional Costume/Props: White button-up shirt, Dark suit, An enamelware pot, Media photos of Oskar Schindler, his factory and/or memorial
Day 5	Game Time	Dodge Ball	10-15 Sponge balls, Goggles for each player, Masking tape, Prizes, Upbeat music (optional)
Bonus	Activity Page	Jesus' Arrest Coloring Sheet	1 Copy for each child

Lesson Introduction:

Gentleness is so needed in our lives. When people allow anger to fly, they are exercising it and making it stronger. So many kids keep anger just under the surface, and they get mad about any little thing. As they exercise gentleness, they can, on purpose, overcome anger.

To say we can't or it's hard says we are trying in our own ability, not walking in God's POWER on the inside. It doesn't mean someone is weak because they don't respond in anger and strife, it means they are obedient and strong.

The Word says in Hebrews that our senses are trained by reason of use. As we exercise gentleness, we will come to the place where no one can "push our buttons" or dictate what we do and feel. A great example of this is a trained lion. He is stronger than his trainer, but he obeys him. We are just like that. Though we could get angry, we choose to be strong in the Lord and walk in gentleness. When we choose to let God exalt us (1 Peter 5:6), we will definitely come out the winner!

Love,

Commander Kellie

Commander Kellie

Lesson Outline:

This week you will teach your children about the fruit of gentleness, also known as *meekness*. Enjoy teaching your children about the strength of this fruit, and help them become the men and women of God they are designed to be.

I. MEEKNESS DOES NOT MEAN WEAKNESS

a. *Weakness* is the inability to defend yourself; *meekness* is putting aside that ability in order to obey God.

b. Jesus knew what God wanted and chose God's will above His own. Matthew 26:39

c. Jesus had <u>plenty</u> of power, yet He wouldn't defend Himself. Matthew 26:53-54

II. GENTLENESS DOES NOT DEMAND ITS OWN WAY

a. We choose His way instead of our own.

b. We are patient with difficult people. 2 Timothy 2:24; Ephesians 4:2

c. We love our enemies and bless when we are cursed. Matthew 5:44

d. Let parents and teachers tell you what to do without arguing back. 1 Peter 5:5

III. THE FRUIT OF GENTLENESS WILL KEEP YOU FROM STRIFE

a. The disciples wanted to fight, but Jesus healed His enemy. Luke 22:49-51

b. Jesus said to turn the other cheek. Let God fight your battles. Matthew 5:39

c. Don't give arguing and strife any place; kick them out! 2 Timothy 2:23-26

d. Gentleness will keep you from striving. Don't get mad, get <u>gentleness!</u>

Notes:

DAY 1: BIBLE LESSON — JESUS' GENTLENESS

 Memory Verse: They must not slander anyone and must avoid quarreling. Instead, they should be gentle and show true humility to everyone. —Titus 3:2

(Corresponds with Lesson Outline No. I-III)

This week's lesson illustrates the strength and courage that gentleness requires. When Jesus was arrested, He could have fought back. He could have called on God's angels to save Him. Instead, He submitted to God's will, knowing the brutality He was about to face. As you study this passage, help your children understand that there is true strength in following God.

Read Matthew 26:47-56:
Jesus Is Betrayed and Arrested

And even as Jesus said this, Judas, one of the twelve disciples, arrived with a crowd of men armed with swords and clubs. They had been sent by the leading priests and elders of the people. The traitor, Judas, had given them a prearranged signal: "You will know which one to arrest when I greet him with a kiss." So Judas came straight to Jesus. "Greetings, Rabbi!" he exclaimed and gave him the kiss.

Jesus said, "My friend, go ahead and do what you have come for."

Then the others grabbed Jesus and arrested him. But one of the men with Jesus pulled out his sword and struck the high priest's slave, slashing off his ear.

"Put away your sword," Jesus told him. "Those who use the sword will die by the sword. Don't you realize that I could ask my Father for thousands of angels to protect us, and he would send them instantly? But if I did, how would the Scriptures be fulfilled that describe what must happen now?"

Then Jesus said to the crowd, "Am I some dangerous revolutionary, that you come with swords and clubs to arrest me? Why didn't you arrest me in the Temple? I was there teaching every day. But this is all happening to fulfill the words of the prophets as recorded in the Scriptures." At that point, all the disciples deserted him and fled.

Discussion Questions:

1. **What happened in this passage?**

2. **When Jesus was arrested, one of the men with Jesus lashed out with his sword. What did Jesus say in response?**

   Jesus told him to put his sword away. He said that if He wanted to, He could ask His Father to send thousands of angels to protect Him.

3. **Why did Jesus respond like that?**

   He knew that this would happen. He had to die in order for the scriptures to be fulfilled so that we could have a relationship with God.

4. **Was this a weak decision or a brave one? Why?**

    It was a brave decision because Jesus could have prevented His own arrest, but He chose to do the right thing. He chose to fulfill His purpose of becoming a sacrifice for humanity.

5. **Can you think of any examples in your life when you have had to choose goodness, even when it's been difficult?**

    Answers will vary.

    Notes:_____

    _____

    _____

    _____

    _____

    _____

    _____

    _____

    _____

    _____

    _____

    _____

    _____

    _____

    _____

    _____

    _____

    _____

    _____

    _____

    _____

    _____

    _____

    _____

DAY 2: ACADEMY LAB — TAKE IT EASY

 Suggested Time: 10 minutes

 Key Scripture: I, too, try to please everyone in everything I do. I don't just do what is best for me; I do what is best for others so that many may be saved. –1 Corinthians 10:33

Supplies: ■ 1 Egg, ■ 4 Eggshell halves, ■ Scissors, ■ Masking tape, ■ Books

(Corresponds to Lesson Outline No. I)

Prior to Lesson:

Create eggshell halves by cracking raw eggs in half. Consider having a few extra eggshells on hand, just in case they are needed.

Prepare the eggshell halves by wrapping a piece of masking tape around the midsection of each empty eggshell half.

With scissors, carefully trim the excess shell so each half has a straight-edged bottom.

Bring the supplies used to create the eggshell halves, so your children can experience what went into the preparation.

Experiment:

After wrapping a piece of masking tape around the midsection of each empty eggshell half and trimming the excess shell to create a straight-edged bottom, lay four eggshell halves dome up, so they form a square.

Place a book on the eggshells. Continue stacking books on top of the first book, until the shells crack. It's surprising how much weight something as fragile as an eggshell can support!

Lesson Instructions:

Today, we're learning about a fruit of the spirit called *gentleness.*

Many times people think that someone who is gentle is easy to take advantage of or weak. We want to show you today that this isn't always true.

I have something in my hand that can seem pretty weak—an egg.

Has anyone ever dropped an egg? What happened?

It broke and splattered all over, right? Well, we have taken some of these "weak" eggshells and prepared them a special way. *(Explain to your children how the eggshells were prepared.)*

Now, we want to show how something that's very fragile can be very strong.

(Demonstrate the strength of the eggshells by placing a book on top of them.)

First Corinthians 10:33 tells us to be considerate of others and to not thoughtlessly hurt those who aren't as free as we are. In other words, be gentle and considerate of others; that way when you tell them about Jesus, they will be ready to listen and not shut you off because you didn't treat them right.

We can take a lesson from these eggshells. They looked weak but turned out to be very strong. Never forget, being gentle doesn't mean being weak, and a gentle person can lead many people to Jesus!

Notes:_____

_____

_____

_____

_____

_____

_____

_____

_____

_____

_____

_____

_____

_____

_____

_____

_____

_____

_____

_____

_____

_____

DAY 3: GIVING LESSON

LAWS ARE GOOD!

 Suggested Time: 10 minutes

 Offering Scripture: Honor God with everything you own; give him the first and the best. Your barns will burst, your wine vats will brim over. –Proverbs 3:9-10 MSG

Supplies: ☐ A police uniform and hat (Consider using a security-guard uniform—one that states authority.)

(Corresponds with Lesson Outline No. I, III)

Lesson Instructions:

(Choose one of your children to assist with the lesson by allowing them to wear the uniform.)

Does anyone know what kind of uniform this is?

Yes! A policeman's.

What is a policeman's job?

(Allow time for your children to share and discuss their ideas.)

Great discussion! A policeman's job is to enforce laws.

Does anyone know what a law is?

Right! A law is established to keep people and property safe.

There are many different types of laws: laws that tell us how to drive, laws that specify the treatment of public property and laws that say where kids can ride their bikes.

Did you know God's Word gives us laws to live by?

Following God's laws helps us lead peaceful and healthy lives.

Let's read our Offering Scripture together from Proverbs 3:9-10. It says, "Honor God with everything you own; give him the first and the best. Your barns will burst, your wine vats will brim over" (MSG).

Now, God doesn't have this rule because He's greedy and wants all your stuff. No, the reason His Word tells us to give the Lord the first and the best is because when we do this, God can give us His best!

Speaking of "best," listen to the second part of God's law: "Your barns will burst, your wine vats will brim over." Now, I know most of you do not have a barn or a wine vat, but what the Bible is saying is that you will be blessed with plenty—not just a little—but with more than you need.

When you follow God's "giving laws," you will be able to bless others. You will be able to help people who do not know about God's laws. You can show someone how generous God is by being generous yourselves. You can even introduce them to our wonderful heavenly Father. How awesome is that?

Variation: Badge

If you don't have access to a uniform, a toy sheriff's or police badge will work well, too!

Notes:_____

_____

_____

_____

_____

_____

_____

_____

_____

_____

_____

_____

_____

_____

_____

_____

_____

_____

_____

_____

_____

_____

_____

_____

_____

_____

_____

_____

_____

DAY 4: REAL DEAL — OSKAR SCHINDLER

 Memory Verse: They must not slander anyone and must avoid quarreling. Instead, they should be gentle and show true humility to everyone.–Titus 3:2

 Concept: Highlighting an interesting historical place, figure or event that illustrates the theme of the day. The theme of the day is gentleness.

 Media: If you have the technical capability, show media photos of Oskar Schindler, his factory and/or memorial. If you do not have this capability, you may print out photos from the Internet to show the kids or check out a book from your local library.

Optional Costume/Props: ■ White button-up shirt, ■ Dark suit, ■ Hair neatly combed, ■ An enamelware pot

(Corresponds with Lesson Outline No. I-III)

Intro:

Today, we are learning about *gentleness.* A powerful leader guides others with a gentle spirit, not with force. Jesus had all the power of heaven, yet chose to be a servant to all. In today's Real Deal, you'll learn about a man who used power and a gentle spirit to serve others.

About Oskar Schindler:

Oskar Schindler was born in Germany in 1908. Mr. Schindler was an ordinary businessman trying to make money. He started out as a salesman, and launched several businesses that failed, leading him to try a career as a German spy. That sounds exciting, but Mr. Schindler ended up in a foreign prison while working as a spy, and was released after World War II began.

In the Money:

The Nazis were a large and powerful German army who believed all Jewish people should be killed. When the Nazis took over Poland, they allowed Mr. Schindler to operate an enamelware business. "Enamelware" is a special kind of cookware. With the help of about 1,000 Jewish workers, who were paid very little, Mr. Schindler created a profitable business.

Mr. Schindler's success in business made him an admired man in the community and with the Nazi soldiers. Soon, Mr. Schindler was invited to special dinner parties with important Nazi leaders. After years of struggling to be successful, Oskar Schindler was finally living the good life!

But, the enjoyment he received from money, success and recognition didn't last long. After seeing a large number of Jewish people killed in a Nazi raid, everything changed for Mr. Schindler.

The Jewish people deserved to be protected and valued. So, at the risk of being thrown into prison or killed, Oskar Schindler began using his enamelware factory to save as many Jewish people as possible.

Pots for People:

Oskar Schindler knew many important Nazi leaders. He convinced the Nazi leaders that many Jewish people were needed to work in his factory.

Because of his charming personality, gentle persuasion and money, Oskar was successful. Even so there were challenges. Two times the Nazis thought they were being tricked (and they were!), so he was thrown into jail. But that didn't keep Mr. Schindler from his mission. After being released, he went back to hiring Jews to help save their lives.

Schindler's Biggest Trick:

After some time, Jewish people could no longer be hired at the enamelware factory, so Oskar Schindler bought another factory to help save more lives.

This factory was designed to make weapons for the Nazis. This presented a dilemma: The factory made weapons for the Nazis, but they would use those weapons to kill more Jewish people. Schindler needed another plan to outsmart the Nazis.

Oskar Schindler decided to make weapons at this factory, with one little catch: none of the weapons would actually work! This plan went well for a while, until Nazi soldiers started complaining about their broken weapons. Oskar had to pay a lot of money to the Nazis to compensate for the faulty equipment.

Down to the Last Dollar:

By the time the war ended, Mr. Schindler had spent his entire fortune on saving the lives of his Jewish workers. Never again would Oskar Schindler have a lot of money; in fact, he had to live with friends because he couldn't afford to live on his own. He also received assistance from Jewish organizations who appreciated his lifesaving efforts.

Oskar Schindler believed there was no price too high, or risk too great, to save lives. He believed it down to his last dollar.

Making History:

Oskar Schindler never intended to be a hero, but he ended up making history by saving the lives of about 1200 Jews. When Oskar Schindler passed away, the Jewish people honored him by burying his body at Mount Zion in Jerusalem. He was awarded the "Righteous Among the Nations" award for saving so many Jewish lives.[1]

Outro:

Oskar Schindler could have used his money and power against the Jewish people, but chose instead to be a gentle and giving servant. That's gentleness and goodness for sure!

This is why Oskar Schindler is today's Real Deal.

---

1   "Oskar Schindler, His List of Life," oskarschindler.com (8/7/2013).

Notes:

DAY 5: GAME TIME

DODGE BALL

Suggested Time: 5-8 minutes

Memory Verse: They must not slander anyone and must avoid quarreling. Instead, they should be gentle and show true humility to everyone. —Titus 3:2

Supplies: ☐ 10-15 Sponge balls, ☐ Goggles for each player, ☐ Prizes, ☐ Upbeat music to play during the game (optional), ☐ Masking tape (to outline the playing court area)

(Corresponds with Lesson Outline No. I-III)

Prior to Game:

This game is best played outdoors.

Identify the area that will serve as the dodge-ball court.

Divide the square in half. The bigger the court, the better!

Game Instructions:

Choose 2 teams with 2-4 players on each team, depending on the size of the dodge-ball court and the number of available players.

Provide each team with an equal amount of sponge balls.

As a rule and for safety, players can only throw the sponge balls below the neck area. The goal of this game is to hit the players on the opposing team with the sponge balls. As soon as a player is hit, they will exit the dodge-ball court.

Playing music during the game will add excitement.

Game Goal:

Be a good shot with the ball, or a quick mover. The last player standing, without being hit by a sponge ball, wins.

Final Word:

A good leader will lead others with a positive example, not with force. It's great to have fun with this game, while recognizing that strength of character is better than one's physical strength.

Notes:_____

_____

_____

_____

_____

_____

_____

_____

_____

_____

_____

_____

_____

_____

_____

_____

_____

_____

_____

_____

_____

_____

_____

_____

_____

_____

_____

_____

_____

_____

_____

_____

_____

_____

_____

_____

_____

ACTIVITY PAGE

JESUS' ARREST COLORING SHEET

 Memory Verse: They must not slander anyone and must avoid quarreling. Instead, they should be gentle and show true humility to everyone. –Titus 3:2

(Corresponds with Lesson Outline No. I-III)

Jesus exhibited great goodness, or meekness, during His life. He chose to obey God, even when it was difficult. At His arrest, He could have defended Himself, but instead, chose to be faithful to God's will.

Notes:

_____

_____

_____

_____

_____

_____

_____

_____

_____

_____

_____

_____

_____

_____

_____

_____

_____

_____

_____

_____

_____

_____

_____

_____

_____

_____

_____

_____

_____

_____

_____

_____

_____

_____

_____

_____

WEEK 11: SELF-CONTROL

 Memory Verse: It teaches us to say "No" to ungodliness and worldly passions, and to live self-controlled, upright and godly lives in this present age. –Titus 2:12 NIV

WEEK 11: SNAPSHOT   SELF-CONTROL

DAY	TYPE OF LESSON	LESSON TITLE	SUPPLIES
Day 1	Bible Lesson	The Temptation of Jesus	None
Day 2	Food Fun	Who Doesn't Like Candy?	1 Resealable plastic food-storage bag, 1 Hammer, 1 Small crockpot (or a microwave oven), 1 Large spoon, 1 Butter knife, Wax paper, 1 Cookie sheet, 1 Serving plate, Disposable gloves, 1 Package of white almond bark, 12 Candy canes or 30-40 peppermint candies (red and green)
Day 3	Giving Lesson	Keep a Secret	Nicely wrapped gift box
Day 4	Storybook Theater	Strawberry Sam	Whiteboard or chalkboard or easel with paper, Dry-erase markers if using whiteboard, Colored chalks if using a chalkboard, Pencil (art pencils work best) and eraser and black marker and rags (to blend chalks) if using paper, Art smock
Day 5	Game Time	Memory Verse Shootout	1 Roll of masking tape, 2 Sponge balls, 2 Cowboy hats, Upbeat music (optional)
Bonus	Activity Page	Jesus' Temptation Look-and-Find	1 Copy for each child

Lesson Introduction:

Many people claim that "Jesus is Lord," but they don't do what He tells them to do. Too many times their flesh gets in the way. But, when they choose to let His Spirit control what they do, then sin is no longer their master (Romans 6:18). Every decision a Superkid makes for the Lord puts his/her spirit man more in charge. That's when they truly do make Jesus the Lord of their lives!

Our flesh wants to take us in the opposite direction of God's instructions. Our kids want to follow the Spirit but can't do it in their flesh—it can't fight itself (Romans 8:9). But, Jesus did the work for us. He paid the price for us to have His strong Spirit on the inside of us, so we won't be weak when temptation to sin comes. We are strong, just like Him!

Love,

Commander Kellie

Commander Kellie

Lesson Outline:

Each of your children is in a battle. The enemy would like nothing better than to convince him/her to go against God's will and follow the flesh. But, as we yield to the Lord's Spirit, we will have the strength to stand firm. Help children understand this and begin to develop their spirit man even more in the coming week.

I. WHO IS IN CHARGE?

a. There is a battle for control over our lives.

b. The Spirit of God gives us the ability to go His direction at all times.

c. <u>Self</u>-control is really <u>God's own</u> self-control within us to have power over our flesh!

II. JESUS WINS A "FLESH BATTLE" Matthew 4:1-11

a. The Holy Spirit came on Jesus. Matthew 3:16-17

b. Satan tries to tempt us to go against God's instructions to us. He tried to get Jesus to sin three times in a row!

c. Jesus had already prepared His heart. It was full of the Word! Psalm 119:11

d. Satan used Peter to tempt Jesus but Jesus didn't let His friend control Him. Mark 8:31-33

III. DON'T LET ANY PART OF YOUR BODY BE USED FOR SIN Romans 6:12-13

a. Without the fruit of self-control, your tongue will be out of control! James 3:2-10

b. Our hands and feet need self-control. 1 Thessalonians 4:11

c. Kids <u>really</u> need self-control in order to obey and honor their parents. Ephesians 6:1-3

d. We have the fruit of self-control inside us. It helps us to not be led by our feelings and emotions. Remember, the fruit of <u>self</u>-control is really <u>God-control</u> within us to have power over our flesh!

Notes:_____

_____

_____

_____

_____

_____

_____

_____

DAY 1: BIBLE LESSON | **THE TEMPTATION OF JESUS**

 Memory Verse: It teaches us to say "No" to ungodliness and worldly passions, and to live self-controlled, upright and godly lives in this present age. —Titus 2:12 NIV

(Corresponds with Lesson Outline No. I-II)

In this passage, Jesus exhibited self-control. When Satan offered Him wealth, power and every fleshly desire, Jesus stood strong. Help train your children to have self-control, too, so that when the enemy tries to entice them, they will stand strong for God.

Read Matthew 4:1-11:
The Temptation of Jesus

Then Jesus was led by the Spirit into the wilderness to be tempted there by the devil. For forty days and forty nights he fasted and became very hungry.

During that time the devil came and said to him, "If you are the Son of God, tell these stones to become loaves of bread."

But Jesus told him, "No! The Scriptures say, 'People do not live by bread alone, but by every word that comes from the mouth of God.'"

Then the devil took him to the holy city, Jerusalem, to the highest point of the Temple, and said, "If you are the Son of God, jump off! For the Scriptures say, 'He will order his angels to protect you. And they will hold you up with their hands so you won't even hurt your foot on a stone.'"

Jesus responded, "The Scriptures also say, 'You must not test the Lord your God.'"

Next the devil took him to the peak of a very high mountain and showed him all the kingdoms of the world and their glory. "I will give it all to you," he said, "if you will kneel down and worship me."

"Get out of here, Satan," Jesus told him. "For the Scriptures say, 'You must worship the Lord your God and serve only him.'"

Then the devil went away, and angels came and took care of Jesus.

Discussion Questions:

1. **Tell me what happened in this passage.**

2. **How did Satan tempt Jesus?**

   Satan tempted Jesus:

   to turn stones into bread

to jump off the mountain and let the angels catch Him

with power and position to rule the world; all He had to do was worship the devil one time

3. **How did Jesus respond to Satan's temptations?**

He responded with the Word and continually reminded Satan that God was supreme.

4. **What does this tell us about how we should respond to temptation?**

We also should respond with the Word.

Notes:_____

_____

_____

_____

_____

_____

_____

_____

_____

_____

_____

_____

_____

_____

_____

_____

_____

_____

_____

_____

_____

_____

_____

_____

_____

_____

_____

DAY 2: FOOD FUN   **WHO DOESN'T LIKE CANDY?**

 Suggested Time: 10 minutes

 Key Scripture: It's not smart to stuff yourself with sweets.... A person without self-control is like a house with its doors and windows knocked out. –Proverbs 25:27-28 MSG

 Mint Party Candy Recipe:

Ingredients: ☐ 1 Package white almond bark, ☐ 6 Candy canes or 15-20 peppermint candies (red and green)

1. Melt 3-4 pieces of almond bark in a crockpot (or microwave oven) until soft enough to stir. (Start this step prior to your lesson so the candy will be ready by lesson time.)
2. Place unwrapped peppermint candies or candy canes in a resealable plastic food-storage bag and crush gently with a hammer.
3. Pour the crushed candy into the melted bark and stir.
4. Place a sheet of wax paper on a cookie sheet.
5. Spread the mixture thinly over the wax paper and place it in a freezer for 5-10 minutes.
6. When the mixture is firm, break the candy into serving-sized pieces.
7. Enjoy!

Supplies: ☐ 1 Resealable plastic food-storage bag, ☐ 1 Hammer, ☐ 1 Small crockpot (or a microwave oven), ☐ 1 Large spoon, ☐ 1 Butter knife, ☐ Wax paper, ☐ 1 Cookie sheet, ☐ 1 Serving plate, ☐ Disposable gloves (used to serve the candy)

(Corresponds with Lesson Outline No. I, III)

Lesson Instructions:

Today, we're making candy, and you're going to be a "sous-chef" (pronounced "sue-chef")! The first step for our sous-chef is to unwrap the peppermint candies and place them in this resealable food storage bag. While that's being prepared, let's check out another important ingredient in the recipe. This is called "almond bark." Great job!

Now, let's crush this candy! *(Gently begin breaking the candy into small pieces inside the food-storage bag with the hammer.)* Would you please now put the crushed candy into the melted almond bark and stir it really well? To complete our recipe, we'll pour the mixture onto the cookie sheet, spread it out to make a thin layer, and place it in the freezer for 5-10 minutes. *(After 10 minutes, remove hardened candy from freezer.)*

Before we can sample this tasty treat, we'll need to break it into serving-sized pieces. I have some of our Mint

Party Candy that has already been hardened, so we have just one more step before it's ready to eat. Let's take a butter knife and break the candy into pieces.

This candy is so yummy, I feel like I could eat the whole batch. Have any of you ever felt that way? How about on special occasions when there are a lot of goodies—are you tempted to just keep eating because it tastes so good? Well, today, we're learning about self-control and in Proverbs 25:27-28 MSG, it says, "It's not smart to stuff yourself with sweets.... A person without self-control is like a house with its doors and windows knocked out." So, enjoy the Mint Party Candy, but don't forget the most important ingredient...self-control!

Notes: _____

_____

_____

_____

_____

_____

_____

_____

_____

_____

_____

_____

_____

_____

_____

_____

_____

_____

_____

_____

_____

_____

_____

_____

DAY 3: GIVING LESSON — KEEP A SECRET

 Suggested Time: 10 minutes

 Offering Scripture: Watch out! Don't do your good deeds publicly, to be admired by others.... Give your gifts in private, and your Father, who sees everything, will reward you. –Matthew 6:1, 4

Supplies: ■ Nicely wrapped gift box

(Corresponds with Lesson Outline No. III)

Lesson Instructions:

How many of you know what it means to keep a secret? What is the worst thing you can do when it comes to secrets? Start telling everyone! Do you see this beautifully wrapped present? No one but me, knows what's inside. It's a secret. That's one thing that makes gifts so much fun—not knowing what's inside—until you open them. It's a secret. Have any of you ever bought a gift and let your little brother or sister, or maybe a friend, see the gift? And THEN, you found out they told someone else about it. I guess that's when we learn who can keep a secret and who can't!

We should never keep secrets from our mom or dad. But, did you know that God says sometimes there is a secret that's good to keep just between you and God? I know, that's pretty surprising, but let's read Matthew 6:1, 4. In these verses, Jesus is telling us to not make a big deal out of our *giving* to try to make people think we're something special. That doesn't mean we sneak up to the offering basket, or try to get people to look away when we put our offering into the basket! But, it does mean we are to try to keep it private between us and the Lord. Only He needs to know what we're giving. When we give this way, we make sure it's all about what's in our hearts, not about what others think. So today, as we prepare our offering for the Lord, make it a BLESSING secret between you and Him!

Notes:_____

_____

_____

_____

_____

_____

_____

_____

_____

DAY 4: STORYBOOK THEATER STRAWBERRY SAM

 Teacher Tip: This segment has many possible variations. Choose the one that best fits your family, and have fun!

List of Characters/Costumes:

- Berries: Use red face paint (from a costume shop) to cover faces, Use black eyeliner to draw seeds on faces, Red T-shirts
- Sam: Red T-shirt and ball cap
- Papa Berry: Red shirt and tie
- Mama Berry: Red blouse and pearls
- Human character: Farmer's straw hat, a plaid shirt and overalls

Supplies: ☐ Whiteboard or chalkboard or easel with paper, ☐ Dry-erase markers if using whiteboard, ☐ Colored chalks if using a chalkboard, ☐ Pencil (art pencils work best) and eraser and colored chalk and black marker and rags (to blend chalks) if using paper, ☐ Art smock (to keep your artist's clothes clean)

(Corresponds with Lesson Outline No. I, III)

Variation No. 1:

Read the story as part of your read-aloud time.

Variation No. 2:

Read the story as an old-time radio skit, complete with different actors for each part. If you are limited on participants, then assign more than one part per person and change the voice. Make copies of the skit, and have each actor highlight his/her lines.

Variation No. 3:

Act out the story as a fun skit. Perhaps your children can practice during the day (even creating fun costumes from everyday items) and then perform it in the evening for the whole family. Before beginning your skit, remember to introduce your cast!

Variation No. 4:

Create a storybook theater where one or more family members sketch the story on a whiteboard, chalkboard or artist's easel as another member reads the story. Initially, there will be a few supplies to purchase but don't let this be a deterrent from using the illustrated story option! Once the supplies have been purchased, they'll be long-lasting and reusable.

To make your presentation easier, lightly sketch the drawing with a pencil prior to presentation. Time may not allow the picture to be completely drawn and colored at the time of the lesson. Erase the pencil lines, so light lines are visible to the artist, but are not obvious to the children. Review the story ahead of time to determine the amount of time needed to complete the illustration while telling the story. When the story begins, use black markers to "draw" the picture, following the sketched pencil lines. Next, apply color using the pastel chalk. Then, blend the color with the rags. Finally, cut the illustration from the board, roll it up and secure it with rubber bands, and share it with one of your children. Or hang the drawing in a central place for the family to enjoy for a few days!

Story:

The first thing you should know about Sam is that he's famous. Now usually, when someone becomes famous, it's because they've done something amazing. Sam certainly accomplished something amazing. My name is Jelani and I live in the middle of an enormous strawberry field. This field is known as Big Patch. Oh, did I mention that Sam is a strawberry? Well, of course he is, or the two of us would never have met. If you promise to listen really closely, I'll tell you the story of Strawberry Sam.

One spring morning when the birds were singing and the sun was shining bright, Sam was born. His parents were very excited to have their first little berry to raise, and they decided to name him Sam. Strawberry Sam, that is.

When Sam sprouted out and lifted his little green head, his mom and dad both gave their biggest smiles and cried out to all the strawberries, "Hey everybody, Strawberry Sam is here, the newest baby berry in Big Patch."

Of course, all the strawberries in the field gave a cheer, like only strawberries can do.

Now, I should explain that humans can't hear a strawberry cheer, it's a special sound reserved only for those who are actually a berry. Don't feel bad, that's just how it is. Now where was I? Oh, yes, the newest berry, little Sam. While everyone was cheering his arrival, Sam's parents noticed something unusual. Sam, who was as green as any little berry should be, was quickly turning red. In fact, the happier and louder the cheering, the redder his face became.

Suddenly, Sam's voice squeaked out, "Stop cheering, everyone! I want peace and quiet, 'cause it's my birthday today!" Slowly, the happy sounds hushed. Sam's mom looked surprised and somewhat embarrassed.

"Sorry, berry friends," she said. "Sam seems to get easily upset."

Once the cheering stopped, and everyone returned to their part of the patch, Sam's face returned to the baby green color it was supposed to be.

Dad Berry turned to Sam's mother and said, "Our baby berry seems to have quite a temper. I guess we will have to keep an eye on that behavior!"

That night, when it was time for bed, all the strawberry parents were extra quiet.

They pulled the night leaves over their little ones and whispered, "Go right to sleep, don't make a peep, nothing will be scary for my little berry."

They whispered because no one wanted Sam to get upset. It was silent all night long.

The next day, life in Big Patch seemed to be back to normal. Sam had actually grown a bit bigger, as berries grow much faster than people. In case you're wondering, being a strawberry is a lot of fun. We get to enjoy a lot of sunshine, and when it gets too hot we just duck under a leaf and cool off with our friends. This is when most berries visit with each other. Strawberries are very talkative, and we like to discuss when we'll be ready to leave Big Patch.

"I want to become part of a strawberry cake," one berry might say.

Another may declare, "I hope to be involved in a fruit cup topped with real whipped cream!"

Sam's parents were no different. They had hopes of Sam joining them in making the perfect strawberry pie. Even Sam agreed that a strawberry pie sounded pretty cool. "I could be the top berry!" he would shout.

"That sounds fine, Sam, but you will have to wait until you're completely ready. No green berries in a pie! Then we can all go together." Sam seemed to like that idea.

As the days went by, Sam grew even bigger. Despite his rough start, he made a lot of friends in Big Patch. Sam was friendly and even funny at times. He told lots of vegetable jokes, which all strawberries find hilarious.

One of Sam's favorite jokes was, "When are vegetables in a bad mood? When they're in a stew about something!"

That joke made the residents of Big Patch laugh every time. Sam's jokes had a way of making everyone feel blessed to be fruit instead of a plain, old veggie.

Although Sam was well-liked and had some good friends, he would get mad at times and lose his temper. One minute, things would be fine, and then something would happen that Sam didn't like. Hoo, boy! Everyone knew when Strawberry Sam was not happy! First of all, his face would become red...very red! Then, Sam would begin shouting and calling other berries mean names. Anyone who was nearby, got an earful. Sam's parents warned him repeatedly that one day his temper would get him in trouble.

"It is not good to say mean things or get angry," said his mother. "We didn't teach you to lose your temper, and you certainly didn't learn that in Smallberry Academy."

Sam's dad would say, "No one's face turns from green to red as quickly as yours. It's supposed to turn red gradually. That's the way a berry stays healthy."

Sam didn't pay too much attention, and his occasional outbursts continued, until one day, that is.

It was a Friday morning, and all the strawberries were waking up and peeking out from under their night leaves.

"I love Fridays," said one berry. "It's the best day of the whole week!"

A voice spoke out from under a large leaf. "Be quiet out there. I'm sleeping in today!"

A few more strawberries emerged. "Ahhh, a beee-u-tiful day!" cried a plump red berry, stretching his stem and turning toward the sun. "I think I'll hang out in this nice sunshine for a while."

A red-faced Sam rose from under his night leaf and glared at the berries. His cheeks were as red as any grown-up strawberry.

"If I hear one more noise, I'm going to be very angry!" shouted Sam. "You'll all be sorry! I'll hide your night leaves! I will never tell another vegetable joke! I'll make you wish you had never...."

All of a sudden, a giant hand reached down and plucked Sam right off the plant. It was a human!

As Sam was being held up in the air, a big booming human voice said, "Why, you're sure a mighty red strawberry. You must be ripe and ready to eat!"

Of course, when Sam heard that, he began to cry as loud as he could, "No, wait, I'm not ripe yet! I just lost my temper. Please don't eat me, I'm just a young strawberry. I'm not ready to leave Big Patch! I'm supposed to be in a strawberry pie with my mom and dad!"

Unfortunately, humans can't hear strawberries, no matter what they might be saying. With that, the human took a big bite out of Strawberry Sam.

Instead of saying, "Oh yeah!" or "Yummy!" he spit Sam out and exclaimed, "Yuk! That little berry is bitter." He threw what was left of Sam far away from the field. All the strawberries in Big Patch looked down with sad faces. Finally, Sam's dad spoke up.

"I guess we all realize how important it is to use self-control with our words and actions."

That night, when the strawberry mommies put their little ones to bed under their warm night leaves, they softly sang, "Go right to sleep, you'll grow up big and sweet, and nothing will be scary, for my little berry." And everyone in Big Patch had sweet sleep.

THE END (of Sam, that is!)

Story by Dana Johnson

Notes:_____

_____

_____

_____

_____

_____

_____

_____

_____

_____

_____

_____

_____

_____

_____

_____

_____

_____

_____

DAY 5: GAME TIME — MEMORY VERSE SHOOTOUT

 Suggested Time: 6-8 minutes

 Memory Verse: It teaches us to say "No" to ungodliness and worldly passions, and to live self-controlled, upright and godly lives in this present age. —Titus 2:12 NIV

 Teacher Tip: For safety, players are only allowed to throw the sponge ball below the neck area of their opponents.

Supplies: ■ 1 Roll of masking tape, ■ 2 Sponge balls, ■ 2 Cowboy hats, ■ Upbeat music to play during game (optional)

(Corresponds with Lesson Outline No. I)

Prior to Game:

Choose 2 players to compete against each other.

Each player will hold a sponge ball and wear a cowboy hat.

Place a tape line on the floor where the players will start and stand back to back.

Players will walk away from each other for a predetermined amount of steps.

Game Instructions:

Share the memory verse, and allow the players to repeat it. Choose 2 players who can say the scripture without assistance and have them stand back to back on the tape line, each with a sponge ball in hand. Players will walk away from each other for a predetermined number of steps while everyone in the room counts out loud. As the children reach the last step, have them turn around and say the memory verse again as quickly as possible, and then throw the sponge ball at their opponent. Players are not allowed to throw the sponge balls until they've finished saying the scripture. The first player to recite the completed memory verse and hit his or her opponent with the sponge ball, wins.

Game Goal:

Be quick to say and know God's Word so you can "shoot" more and "hit the mark" the most times to win!

Final Word:

There's a battle going on every day for control of our lives. It's like a shootout between our flesh and our spirits. Self-control helps us win that battle every time!

Notes:_____

_____

_____

_____

_____

_____

_____

_____

_____

_____

_____

_____

_____

_____

_____

_____

_____

_____

_____

_____

_____

_____

_____

_____

_____

_____

_____

_____

_____

_____

_____

_____

_____

_____

ACTIVITY PAGE

JESUS' TEMPTATION LOOK-AND-FIND

Memory Verse: It teaches us to say "No" to ungodliness and worldly passions, and to live self-controlled, upright and godly lives in this present age. –Titus 2:12 NIV

(Corresponds with Lesson Outline No. II)

Jesus turned down the devil's temptations and remained faithful to God. He may have been tempted, but He saw the truth of just how empty Satan's promises were. His self-control was developed enough so He could withstand the pressure. Find the 13 items listed below that are hidden within the picture.

Answer Key:

Notes:_____

_____

_____

_____

_____

_____

_____

_____

_____

_____

_____

WEEK 12: GET DRESSED!

 Memory Verse: *Since God chose you to be the holy people he loves, you must clothe yourselves with tender-hearted mercy, kindness, humility, gentleness, and patience.* –Colossians 3:12

WEEK 12: SNAPSHOT — GET DRESSED!

DAY	TYPE OF LESSON	LESSON TITLE	SUPPLIES
Day 1	Bible Lesson	Everything for Godly Living	None
Day 2	Read-Aloud	Flesh Guy vs. Spirit Guy	None
Day 3	Giving Lesson	Do the Right Thing	A basket of fruit (real or plastic), 1 Stuffed-toy lamb, A wooden stick or rod, A fake beard, A white robe
Day 4	Object Lesson	The Right Outfit	A fun, goofy outfit: (ex: wig, glasses, shirt, brightly colored tie, big baggy pants, galoshes, etc.), A large shopping bag
Day 5	Game Time	Trash Bash	1 Roll of masking tape, 1 Large trash bag full of wadded-up paper balls, A stopwatch, timer or watch with a second hand, Upbeat music (optional)
Bonus	Activity Page	Fruit of the Spirit Acrostic	1 Copy for each child

Lesson Introduction:

Remind your Superkids what it was like when they learned to dress themselves. At first, they probably went out without clothes on at all and didn't even care! They had to be taught, reminded over and over again and finally, after daily practice, they began looking pretty good on the outside.

This is a great picture of the way many Christians live their lives—they are naked. They live without their Spirit-Guy clothing (fruit) from the inside, manifest on the outside. Paul phrased it that we are to "clothe ourselves" because we must choose to put on the outside what is on the inside. I'm sure that today, all your children are fully clothed with physical clothing, and no one has forgotten to get dressed! The nature of God, our "super-hero" suit, works exactly the same way. Just as with our physical clothing, the more we practice putting on our spiritual "clothing" <u>every day,</u> the more natural, effortless and part of us it becomes!

Love,

Commander Kellie

Commander Kellie

Lesson Outline:

Each of God's people makes a choice every day: Will we be led by the Spirit or by our flesh? Your children are no different. Every day they make the choice to walk in the spirit and reflect God's nature, or walk in the flesh and live self-centered, carnal lives. Help your children make the right choice—the choice to live a life full of the fruit of the spirit. When they do, they'll be a blessing to the Lord and to those around them!

I. NEVER FORGET WHO YOU ARE 2 Peter 1:3-9

a. You contain ALL of God, not just a little bit—100 percent of God is in you!

b. To be godly requires a quality decision to wear His clothes (fruit of the spirit)!

c. Christians who don't walk in the spirit forget they've been changed. 2 Peter 1:9

II. FLESH GUY VS. SPIRIT GUY, A SUPERHERO BATTLE

a. Your old self (Flesh Guy) wants to call the shots. Most people think he is the strongest and you can't beat him.

b. Take off the old, dirty Flesh Guy clothes and trash them. Romans 13:12-14

c. Don't spend time thinking of ways to feed Flesh Guy. Starve him out!

d. Exercise Spirit Guy and he will become "Superhero Champion"!

III. GETTING DRESSED IS SOMETHING WE ALL HAVE TO LEARN AND PRACTICE

a. Toddlers have to learn to dress themselves. Sometimes they forget!

b. Any fruit of the spirit that's missing is like being partially dressed.

c. People need to see your fruit, not your flesh. Colossians 3:17

d. As you stay in Him, you'll produce lots of fruit! John 15:7-8

Notes:_____

_____

_____

_____

_____

_____

_____

DAY 1: BIBLE LESSON | **EVERYTHING FOR GODLY LIVING**

 Memory Verse: *Since God chose you to be the holy people he loves, you must clothe yourselves with tenderhearted mercy, kindness, humility, gentleness, and patience.* –Colossians 3:12

(Corresponds with Lesson Outline No. I-II)

Over the last several weeks, your children have learned about the fruit of the spirit. This week, you'll be helping them put what they've learned into action. They'll learn that by relying on the Holy Spirit and choosing to walk according to God's Word, life will be so much more rewarding.

Read 2 Peter 1:3-9:
Growing in Faith

By his divine power, God has given us everything we need for living a godly life. We have received all of this by coming to know him, the one who called us to himself by means of his marvelous glory and excellence. And because of his glory and excellence, he has given us great and precious promises. These are the promises that enable you to share his divine nature and escape the world's corruption caused by human desires.

In view of all this, make every effort to respond to God's promises. Supplement your faith with a generous provision of moral excellence, and moral excellence with knowledge, and knowledge with self-control, and self-control with patient endurance, and patient endurance with godliness, and godliness with brotherly affection, and brotherly affection with love for everyone.

The more you grow like this, the more productive and useful you will be in your knowledge of our Lord Jesus Christ. But those who fail to develop in this way are shortsighted or blind, forgetting that they have been cleansed from their old sins.

Discussion Questions:

1. **According to this passage, what has God given us to live a godly life?**

   God has given us everything we need to live a godly life.

2. **What does it mean to you to live a godly life?**

   Answers will vary, but use this time to make sure your children have a clear understanding of what it means to live a godly life.

3. **How did we receive the ability to live a godly life?**

   We received the ability to live a godly life through Jesus.

How does this passage tell us to supplement our faith?

It tells us to supplement, or add to, our faith with moral excellence (ethical, or right, living), knowledge, self-control, patience, godliness, brotherly affection (kindness) and love.

4. **Why is it important to supplement our faith like this?**

We become more useful to the Lord and the Body of Christ. God is able to use us to bless and help His people.

Notes:_____

_____

_____

_____

_____

_____

_____

_____

_____

_____

_____

_____

_____

_____

_____

_____

_____

_____

_____

_____

_____

_____

_____

_____

_____

DAY 2: READ-ALOUD

FLESH GUY VS. SPIRIT GUY

 Suggested Time: 15 minutes

 Memory Verse: *Since God chose you to be the holy people he loves, you must clothe yourselves with tenderhearted mercy, kindness, humility, gentleness, and patience.* –Colossians 3:12

(Corresponds to Lesson Outline No. II)

Background:

Today, your children will meet Toby, an average teenager who is in a battle between Spirit Guy and Flesh Guy. Help your children see that, like Toby, they make Spirit Guy and Flesh Guy choices every day.

Story:

Toby, a teenager, was asleep in his bed. He had no idea that a battle was about to begin in his room. On one side was Flesh Guy, off to the side asleep and snoring. On the other side was Spirit Guy, reading his Bible.

"Toby, time to wake up!" his mother called from the kitchen.

Toby grunted and buried his head in his pillow.

Flesh Guy whined. "That's it, Toby, don't move. I'm still tired."

But Spirit Guy spoke up, "Remember, Toby, the joy of the Lord is your strength! How about some praise-and-worship music to get you going?"

Suddenly Toby sat up. "That's a good idea. I've wanted to listen to my Superkid CD again." He pushed out of bed and began flipping through his CDs.

Flesh Guy continued to whine. "You just had to open your big mouth, didn't you? Thanks to you, I just missed out on 15 more minutes of sleep. Come to think of it, you did that yesterday too. I've about had it with you, Spirit Guy!"

Spirit Guys smiled. "Don't be angry, Flesh Guy. I promise, if you'll just listen to me..."

"If I just listen to you, I'll never sleep again!" Flesh Guy glared at his opponent and clenched his fists. "Come on, put 'em up."

Spirit Guy shook his head and then rose to direct Toby toward a pile of stuff where he'd find his CD.

"Oh, there it is," Tody smiled. "Thanks, Lord!"

"Way to be thankful, Toby, ol' buddy!" Spirit Guy said, giving him a thumbs up.

Flesh Guy acted like he was gagging himself with his finger. "Yeah, yeah. Big deal. He found a CD. Yippee. Can we get some food sometime this year? I'm starving."

Toby stood up straight. "Wow, I'm hungry." Then he yelled out. "Mom, what's for breakfast?"

"Oatmeal with blueberries," his mom called back.

Flesh Guy scowled. "Yuck. I hate oatmeal and blueberries. It's so...healthy. Hey, Toby, you had some leftover chips and a candy bar in your backpack. Just eat that, and then you can say you're not hungry! You wouldn't even be lying."

Toby grabbed his backpack and started digging inside until he found what he was looking for. "They're kind of smashed, but oh well..." He inspected the nearly flat chocolate bar and then ripped the wrapper and took a bite.

Flesh Guy started dancing a victory dance around Spirit Guy. "Ha, ha, ha, ha, ha, ha. Loser!"

Spirit Guy moved past him to reach Toby. "But Toby, that junk food is no good for you. You need to treat your body right. After all, it's the house of the Holy Spirit."

"Maybe it would be a good idea to eat some oatmeal. I do have a big game today, and it probably isn't smart to eat this junk." Toby threw the chocolate bar away and left the room. A few minutes later he returned with a bowl of oatmeal.

"All right, that's it!" Flesh Guy fumed. "Nobody takes away my junk food AND gets away with it. Nobody!"

Toby took a bite and made a little face.

"Ugh!" Flesh Guy choked. "Why are you doing this to me?!"

Spirit Guy cheered. "Good job, Toby." Flesh Guy tried to punch him, but missed, while Toby kept eating.

"You know, Toby, this would be the perfect time to read your Bible before school. No distractions." Spirit Guy handed Toby his Bible.

"Ha! Distractions galore, coming right up!" Flesh Guy brought over a comic book.

"Oh, man! I forgot about this comic book. This one is awesome." Toby set the Bible aside and grabbed the comic book.

Suddenly Flesh Guy pushed Spirit Guy to the floor and smacked him on top of the head. "That'll teach you to make me get up early and eat oatmeal! I'm in charge today, Spirit Guy. And if things keep going the way I've planned, I'll be in charge EVERY day! Ha, ha, ha, ha, ha."

Spirit Guy rubbed his head. "I don't think so, Flesh Guy. Toby listens to the Holy Spirit. It's just a matter of time before he sees right through your plan!"

Toby set down the comic book and paused for a moment. "You're right, Holy Spirit. I need to build up my Spirit Guy instead of feeding my Flesh Guy. Jesus, I'm putting You first today. And You said that when I put You first, things will work out great for me. So that means today is going to be a great day!" Toby grabbed his Bible and began reading.

Spirit Guy got up and flexed his muscles. He pointed at Flesh Guy to sit down. Flesh Guy reluctantly obeyed. "Yep, that's right, Flesh Guy. Not another word."

Discussion Questions:

Use these questions as conversation starters. Enjoy this time of conversation with your children.

1. Can you tell me what happened in this story?

2. Is there really a Flesh Guy and Spirit Guy? Explain.

3. Has there ever been a battle inside you between Flesh Guy and Spirit Guy, when you knew the right thing to do, but wanted to do your own thing, instead?

4. Who had Toby's best interests at heart?

5. Can you give me examples of things that Flesh Guy would tell *you* to do? Things Spirit Guy would tell you to do?

Notes:_____

_____

_____

_____

_____

_____

_____

_____

_____

_____

_____

_____

_____

_____

_____

_____

_____

_____

_____

_____

_____

_____

_____

_____

DAY 3: GIVING LESSON DO THE RIGHT THING

 Suggested Time: *10 minutes*

 Offering Scripture: *God spoke to Cain: "Why this tantrum? Why the sulking? If you do well, won't you be accepted?"* –Genesis 4:6-7 MSG

Supplies: ☐ *A basket of fruit (real or plastic),* ☐ *1 Stuffed-toy lamb,* ☐ *A wooden stick or rod,* ☐ *A fake beard,* ☐ *A white robe*

(Corresponds with Lesson Outline No. II)

Prior to Lesson:

Have three volunteers, if possible. Scatter the fruit around the stage or presentation area.

One volunteer (Cain) will hold the basket; the next volunteer (Abel) will hold the stuffed-toy lamb and wooden stick or rod; and the third volunteer will play the part of God, wearing the fake beard and white robe.

Lesson Instructions:

There were two brothers, one named Cain, and the other, Abel. Each had a job: Cain worked in the fields growing fruits, vegetables and wheat. *(Have "Cain" pick up the fruit and put it in his basket.)* Abel took care of sheep. *(Have "Abel" pet his lamb, talk to it; have fun with this!)*

Both brothers decided to give an offering to God. Cain brought fruits and vegetables for his offering, while Abel brought a lamb from the firstborn of his flock. *("Cain" and "Abel" present their offerings to "God.")* The Lord respected the offering from Abel, but not the offering from Cain. Cain became very upset. *("Cain" looks angry and pouts.)* The Lord said to Cain, "Why are you throwing a tantrum? Why are you pouting? If you do the right thing, won't you be accepted too?"

Why did God not accept Cain's offering? *(Allow time for your children to share and discuss their ideas.)* When we bring our offerings to God, the most important thing He looks at is our hearts—the attitude we have when we're giving. It's obvious to see that Cain's problem was his attitude because of the way he reacted when God didn't accept his gift. He even stayed angry when God gave him a second chance to change his attitude and bring his offering the right way.

Today, as we prepare to bring our offerings to the Lord, let's make sure we're like Abel, who brought his offering with a right heart!

Notes:_____

_____

_____

DAY 4: OBJECT LESSON | THE RIGHT OUTFIT |

 Suggested Time: *10 minutes*

 Memory Verse: *Get out of bed and get dressed! Don't loiter and linger, waiting until the very last minute. Dress yourselves in Christ, and be up and about!* –Romans 13:14 MSG

Supplies: ■ A fun, goofy outfit: (ex: a wig, glasses, shirt, brightly colored tie, big baggy pants, galoshes, etc.), ■ A large shopping bag in which to bring the costume

(Corresponds with Lesson Outline No. III)

Lesson Instructions:

Today, I have something fun to show you but I need you to help me out. Do I have a volunteer? Now that my wonderful helper is here, we can get started. By the way, would you like to be my helper today and model some of the things I bought?

The other day I was out doing one of my favorite things—shopping—and did I ever run into some fabulous bargains! I thought it would be fun to have my volunteer model all the wonderful things I bought. Let's see, where do I start? *(Begin pulling out the pieces and have your helper put them on one by one. Take your time and make a big deal out of how great he/she looks.)* You know, I think my model looks awesome!

What do you think, kids? Oh! You don't like the outfit? So, you don't think I did a very good job in dressing him/her? Well, this actually reminds me of a scripture in Romans 13:14 MSG. It says, "Get out of bed and get dressed.... Dress yourselves in Christ, and be up and about!" Did you know there are kids—even big kids— who let someone else dress them every day?

Your "spirit man," the real you who lives inside you, needs to get dressed every day. But, if you don't dress your own spirit, the devil will. He'll try to put a "bad attitude" on your heart, or maybe disobedience or resentment. He might also try to get your "spirit man" to wear a bad temper or tell a lie. Let's listen to this verse again; it says, "Dress <u>yourselves</u> in Christ."

We're supposed to dress ourselves, not let the devil do it. And, it even tells us what to wear, but not this goofy outfit! We're supposed to put on Jesus. Now that's an outfit we can be proud of!

Notes:_____

_____

_____

_____

_____

_____

DAY 5: GAME TIME

TRASH BASH

 Suggested Time: 10-15 minutes

 Memory Verse: *Since God chose you to be the holy people he loves, you must clothe yourselves with tenderhearted mercy, kindness, humility, gentleness, and patience.* –Colossians 3:12

Supplies: ☐ 1 Roll of masking tape, ☐ 1 Large trash bag full of wadded-up paper balls, ☐ A stopwatch, timer or watch with a second hand, ☐ Upbeat music to play during the game (optional)

(Corresponds with Lesson Outline No. I)

Prior to Game:

Tape a large box shape on the floor. Empty the trash bag full of paper balls outside the box. Divide players into 2 teams. Position team 1 inside the box and team 2 outside the box.

Game Instructions:

When the timer starts, team 2 will throw the paper balls into the box area as fast as they can, as team 1 throws the paper balls back out. Teams are not allowed to cross the tape lines or engage in physical contact with the opposing team at any time during the game. Allow the "Trash Bash" to last for about 30 seconds. Count the paper balls inside the box area, then allow teams to trade places and repeat the game.

Game Goal:

The team in the box with the least amount of paper balls in the box, wins!

Final Word:

Be sure and keep the trash out of your life. Don't let someone else dirty up your "house"! After all, God lives in you!

Notes:_____

_____

_____

_____

_____

_____

ACTIVITY PAGE

FRUIT OF THE SPIRIT ACROSTIC

Memory Verse: *Since God chose you to be the holy people he loves, you must clothe yourselves with tenderhearted mercy, kindness, humility, gentleness, and patience.* –Colossians 3:12

(Corresponds with Lesson Outline I-III)

Over the last several weeks, you've studied the fruit of the spirit. Use all you've learned to unscramble these words. To decipher the final phrase, copy the letters in the numbered spaces into the spaces at the bottom of the page with the same number.

RITYLAOM

DEGNELOWK

ELFS-NLORTCO

TIAPEECN

SLINEGSDO

NEKSDINS

VELO

YJO

CAPEE

NOSOGEDS

FLISATHFUNES

GELTNSESEN

ANSWER KEY:

RITYLAOM	MORALITY
DEGNELOWK	KNOWLEDGE
ELFS-NLORTCO	SELF-CONTROL
TIAPEECN	PATIENCE
SLINEGSDO	GODLINESS
NEKSDINS	KINDNESS
VELO	LOVE
YJO	JOY
CAPEE	PEACE
NOSOGEDS	GOODNESS
FLISATHFUNES	FAITHFULNESS
GELTNSESEN	GENTLENESS

JESUS IS LORD
OF MY LIFE

Notes:

WEEK 13: COMMUNION

 Memory Verse: This is my body which is given for you. Do this to remember me. –1 Corinthians 11:24

WEEK 13: SNAPSHOT COMMUNION

DAY	TYPE OF LESSON	LESSON TITLE	SUPPLIES
Day 1	Bible Lesson	Communion	None
Day 2	Object Lesson	Bread and Blood	1 Goblet (or glass) of grape juice, A large round uncut loaf of French bread, 1 Water balloon, A small container of red food coloring, 1 Serrated knife, A clear platter
Day 3	Giving Lesson	Make Them Count	5 Different containers: 4 Containers with contents and 1 empty container (ex: A bottle of juice, a box of cereal, a clear empty glass, etc.)
Day 4	Storybook Theater	The Best Sticky Note	Whiteboard, chalkboard or easel with paper, Dry-erase markers if using whiteboard, Colored chalks if using a chalkboard, Pencil (art pencils work best) and eraser and black marker and rags (to blend chalks) if using paper, Art smock (to keep your artist's clothes clean), see page 219 for optional costumes and props
Day 5	Game Time	Hula-Hoop® Thread	2 Hula Hoops®, Small prizes, Upbeat music (optional)
Bonus	Activity Page	Last Supper Color-by-Number	1 Copy for each child

Lesson Introduction:

This lesson is a very basic teaching on Communion. I wrote this as an initial introduction to the concept of what Jesus paid for, and our obligation to remember. I realize much more can be taught and said on this subject. Feel free to expound depending on the level of your group. I would emphasize that Jesus bought us the most valuable supply of treasures.

By remembering what He did, we honor Him. Our faith in His purchase grows through our obedience. Be sure to create an atmosphere of honor and respect when you take Communion with the kids, but do not let it become religious. Let what Jesus did for us get your full attention during this most momentous experience with your children!

Final thought: *We receive Communion to remember what Jesus did!*

Love,

Commander Kellie

Commander Kellie

Lesson Outline:

Communion is such a special time of remembering what Jesus did. The Word tells us that His body was broken so our bodies could be whole, and His blood was shed so our spirits could be free from sin.

As you teach this lesson, be sure to communicate to your children how grateful you are for all the Lord has done for you personally. Be transparent and sincere. You have been saved and set free. And, so have your children! Now, that's something to celebrate. Praise God!

I. JESUS HAD A MOST UNUSUAL DINNER RESERVATION Mark 14:12-25

    a. He told His disciples to follow a man carrying water.

    b. Complete strangers gave them what they needed!

    c. A private room had been prepared for them.

II. THE DISCIPLES GET SOME UNUSUAL INSTRUCTIONS

    a. While they were eating, Jesus held up the bread and wine.

    b. He told them that the bread and wine were His body and blood.

    c. The disciples did not understand that Jesus would die for them.

III. JESUS PAID FOR EVERYTHING 1 Corinthians 11:24; Matthew 26:28

    a. Jesus' body was broken so our bodies could be whole.

    b. Jesus' blood was shed so our spirits could be free from sin.

    c. We need to remember what our Lord did for us. 1 Corinthians 11:25

Notes:_____

_____

_____

_____

_____

_____

_____

_____

_____

DAY 1: BIBLE LESSON — COMMUNION

 Memory Verse: *This is my body, which is given for you. Do this to remember me.* –1 Corinthians 11:24

(Corresponds with Lesson Outline No. I-III)

We end this volume of the *Superkid Home Bible Study* with the study of Communion. Communion is a special time of remembering all Jesus did for us. As this study comes to a close, celebrate the growth your children have experienced over the past 13 weeks and the work the Lord is doing in their lives.

Read Mark 14:12-25:
The Last Supper

On the first day of the Festival of Unleavened Bread, when the Passover lamb is sacrificed, Jesus' disciples asked him, "Where do you want us to go to prepare the Passover meal for you?"

So Jesus sent two of them into Jerusalem with these instructions: "As you go into the city, a man carrying a pitcher of water will meet you. Follow him. At the house he enters, say to the owner, 'The Teacher asks: Where is the guest room where I can eat the Passover meal with my disciples?' He will take you upstairs to a large room that is already set up. That is where you should prepare our meal." So the two disciples went into the city and found everything just as Jesus had said, and they prepared the Passover meal there.

In the evening Jesus arrived with the twelve disciples. As they were at the table eating, Jesus said, "I tell you the truth, one of you eating with me here will betray me."

Greatly distressed, each one asked in turn, "Am I the one?"

He replied, "It is one of you twelve who is eating from this bowl with me. For the Son of Man must die, as the Scriptures declared long ago. But how terrible it will be for the one who betrays him. It would be far better for that man if he had never been born!"

As they were eating, Jesus took some bread and blessed it. Then he broke it in pieces and gave it to the disciples, saying, "Take it, for this is my body."

And he took a cup of wine and gave thanks to God for it. He gave it to them, and they all drank from it. And he said to them, "This is my blood, which confirms the covenant between God and his people. It is poured out as a sacrifice for many. I tell you the truth, I will not drink wine again until the day I drink it new in the Kingdom of God."

Discussion Questions:

1. **What happened in this passage?**

2. **This passage may remind you of something special that we do in our church on occasion. Can you tell me what it is?**

   Communion.

3. **Why is Communion so important?**

   Communion reminds us of Jesus' sacrifice. He paid the price for our sin so we could know the Father.

4. **A *covenant* is a binding agreement, a type of contract, between the Lord and His people. The old covenant involved the shedding of the blood of an animal. In this passage, Jesus says that His blood (the blood that would be shed on the cross) would bring about a new covenant, a new agreement or type of contract, between God and His people. What do you think this means?**

   Parents, talk to your children about the new life we have in Christ. There are many aspects of this that you may choose to address:

   - Through Jesus' death, we are no longer under the Law but, instead, under grace. We are forgiven for the wrong things we have done.

   - Through Jesus' death, we can talk directly to God. We don't have to talk to God through a priest.

   - Through Jesus' death, God's family now includes both Hebrews and gentiles. We have been adopted into the family, and the blessings of Deuteronomy 28 are now ours, too.

   - Because of Jesus' death, we have the Holy Spirit living inside us, so we have the Comforter with us always.

5. **Do you have any questions about Communion?**

   Questions will vary. Answer accordingly.

6. **What are you thankful for about what Jesus did for us and the new covenant that we enjoy with our heavenly Father? Parents, share your own testimonies of gratitude.**

   Answers will vary.

Variation: Communion

Invite your children to help you plan a special dinner (perhaps even a traditional Passover feast). End the evening taking Communion together as a family.

Notes:_____

_____

_____

_____

_____

_____

_____

_____

_____

_____

_____

DAY 2: OBJECT LESSON | **BREAD AND BLOOD**

 Suggested Time: 10 minutes

 Key Scripture: As they were eating, Jesus took some bread and blessed it. Then he broke it in pieces and gave it to the disciples, saying, "Take it, for this is my body." –Mark 14:22

Supplies: ☐ 1 Goblet (or glass) of grape juice, ☐ A large round uncut loaf of French bread, ☐ 1 Water balloon, ☐ A small container of red food coloring, ☐ 1 Serrated knife (butter knife will work if it will cut through the bread and balloon), ☐ A clear platter

(Corresponds to Lesson Outline No. I-III)

Prior to Segment:

Turn the loaf of bread upside down and pull a piece of bread from the middle. (Keep from tearing a hole in the top of the loaf.)

As this lesson is shared with your children, place a few drops of the red food coloring and water in the water balloon and place it inside the bread.

While sharing the lesson, cut through the bread to where the balloon has been placed to illustrate the blood being shed from Jesus' body while He was hanging on the cross.

Lesson Instructions:

Today, we are learning about something very important. In fact, it was one of the last things Jesus did before He was crucified. He had a very special dinner with His disciples. It would be the last time that they all sat down and ate together before He died.

I don't know everything they had for dinner that night, but I do know the two most important parts of their meal: They had wine to drink *(hold up the goblet of juice)*, and they had some bread *(show the French bread)*. The reason these two parts of the dinner were so important is because they stood for something. Jesus told them the wine stood for His blood that would pour out of His cuts and wounds when He hung on the cross. And, there was something special about the bread, too. In Mark 14:22 it says, "As they were eating, Jesus took some bread and blessed it. Then he broke it in pieces and gave it to the disciples, saying, 'Take it, for this is my body.'"

Let me give you a little picture of what it was like: There they were, all sitting at the table, and Jesus took hold of the bread *(take the bread and knife)*. In those days, they didn't cut the bread, they tore off the amount they wanted in chunks. As Jesus tore the bread, He told them that the bread was like His body that was going to be "torn up." It would be cut and bleeding, bruised and hurting. *(Cut into the bread, and as you do cut through the balloon so the red water flows out.)* Jesus wanted to give the disciples a picture that would stick in their minds. He didn't want them to ever forget the torture He would go through for them. Why? They needed to know He was willing to put up with the pain so they could be well in their bodies.

Kids, there was no blood that ran out of the bread when Jesus tore it into pieces. But just like Jesus wanted the disciples to always remember what His body went through for them, He wants to put a picture in your minds, too. Don't ever forget what Jesus went through so you and I can live without sin, sickness and disease.

(Lead the kids in thanking Jesus for what He took for us. Have them repeat after you.) Jesus, You're so amazing! Jesus, thank You for letting Your body be injured so mine could be well. Thank You for giving Your blood so my heart could be clean. I will always remember to say thank You!

Notes:_____

DAY 3: GIVING LESSON | **MAKE THEM COUNT**

 Suggested Time: 10 minutes

 Offering Scripture: It's your heart, not the dictionary, that gives meaning to your words.... Words are powerful; take them seriously. –Matthew 12:34, 36 MSG

Supplies: ■ 5 Different containers: 4 Containers with contents and 1 empty container (ex: A bottle of juice, a box of cereal, a clear empty glass, etc.)

(Corresponds with Lesson Outline No. II)

Prior to Lesson:

Begin by setting out your containers on a table in the front of the room.

Lesson Instructions:

On this table are five different items. Can anyone tell me what they all have in common? *(Allow time for your children to share their ideas.)* They're all containers, and they each contain something different. The Bible teaches us about another container. In Matthew 12:34, it says, "It's your heart, not the dictionary, which gives meaning to your words." Verse 36 says, "Words are powerful; take them seriously."

What kind of container is this scripture referring to? Yes! It's our words! Our words are containers, and they can hold all kinds of things: love, hate, fear, faith, etc. Remember, the scripture we just read said our words are powerful and we need to take them seriously. So today, before we bring our offering to the Lord, let's use these powerful containers called words and pray together.

Say this with me: "Father God, I bring my offering to You today with words of faith. I believe Your Word is true and when I give, You will bless me. I want You to know that I'm preparing my offering for You today because I love You and appreciate everything You have done for me. Thank You for being such an amazing heavenly Father. Holy Spirit, help me use my 'word containers' in the right way. In Jesus' Name. Amen."

Notes:_____

_____

_____

_____

_____

_____

DAY 4: STORYBOOK THEATER

THE BEST STICKY NOTE

Teacher Tip: This segment has many possible variations. Choose the one that best fits your family, and have fun!

List of Characters/Optional Costumes/Props:

- *Geno: T-shirt and ball cap*
- *Sister: messy hair*

Supplies: ☐ Whiteboard, chalkboard or easel with paper, ☐ Dry-erase markers if using whiteboard, colored chalks if using chalkboard, or pencil (art pencils work best) and eraser, black marker and rags (to blend chalks) if using paper, ☐ Art smock (to keep your artist's clothes clean)

(Corresponds with Lesson Outline No. II, III)

Variation No. 1:

Read the story as part of your read-aloud time.

Variation No. 2:

Read the story as an old-time radio skit, complete with different actors for each part. If you are limited on participants, then assign more than one part per person and change the voice. Make copies of the skit and have each actor highlight his/her lines.

Variation No. 3:

Act out the story as a fun skit. Perhaps your children can practice during the day (even creating fun costumes from everyday items) and then perform it in the evening before the whole family. Before beginning your skit, remember to introduce your cast!

Variation No. 4:

Create a storybook theater where one or more family members sketch the story on a whiteboard, chalkboard or artist's easel as another member reads the story. Initially, there will be a few supplies to purchase but don't let this be a deterrent from using the illustrated story option! Once the supplies have been purchased, they'll be long-lasting and reusable.

To make your presentation easier, lightly sketch the drawing with a pencil prior to presentation. Time may not allow the picture to be completely drawn and colored at the time of the lesson. Erase the pencil lines, so light lines are visible to the artist, but are not obvious to your children. Review the story ahead of time to determine the amount of time needed to complete the illustration while telling the story. When the story begins, use black markers to "draw" the picture, following the sketched pencil lines. Next, apply color using the pastel chalk. Then, blend the color with the rags. Finally, cut the illustration from the board, roll it up, secure it with rubber bands, and share it with one of your children!

Story:

For as long as he could remember, Geno's mom had left him notes. Not your ordinary, everyday notes, *sticky notes!* Every place in Geno's house had a sticky note on it at one time or another. In fact, every morning when he woke up, the first thing he saw was a sticky note. Geno slept on the lower level of a bunk bed that he had all to himself, and his mom always left a note stuck above his head, so he would see it when he opened his eyes. This morning was no different.

He looked up. Sure enough, the note was there, waiting for him: "Remember to get your lunch out of the refrigerator."

Geno sat up, gave a good stretch, and walked over to his dresser to get a pair of jeans. "Remember to put your pj's away."

Obeying his second note of the day, Geno opened the dresser drawer and stuffed his pajamas inside. Walking into the bathroom, he looked at the mirror: "Don't forget to brush your teeth and put the lid on the toothpaste."

Geno took the toothpaste lid off and smeared a bit of toothpaste on the note. "Now it's a real sticky note," he said to himself, smiling into the mirror.

Brushing teeth wasn't Geno's favorite thing, so he usually brushed as quickly as possible. That is, unless his mom was watching. He liked to imagine the toothbrush was a race car skimming across his teeth, lightning fast.

"On your mark, get set, GO!"

In about 15 seconds, Geno had dragged the toothbrush across his teeth and spit in the sink. "We have a winner!" he declared.

He reached for the sink handle to rinse away the extra globs of toothpaste and spied a shiny, little piece of paper stuck underneath the foamy glob. He poised two fingers to scoop it up, but it wouldn't budge.

"Trying to mess with me, huh? You're coming off, all right."

This time he tried a different approach. Geno turned the water on full blast. Water sprayed all over, soaking his shirt and the mirror, and sending a Niagara Falls-like mist into the air. Still stuck.

"This is ridiculous!" he exclaimed.

Now the little paper was starting to aggravate Geno. He stared it down, like an Old West cowboy ready to fight a duel. By now, the paper no longer had toothpaste all over it, and he could see what it was. Sure enough, it was another sticky note.

"It must have fallen off the mirror into the sink. That's weird, it's not even wet, and the ink didn't smear."

Geno scratched his fingernail across the note, and it squeaked. It was shiny and slick, like plastic. He scratched his head and wrinkled his nose, trying to figure out this strange new sticky note. And why wouldn't it come off the sink? Two minutes ago Geno felt like a cowboy, but had quickly morphed into a detective trying to solve a mystery.

"Think, Geno, think," he said to himself. "What's slick, shiny, can keep dry and sticks?"

His sister knocked on the door. "Are you almost finished? I need to fix my hair. I'm leaving in 10 minutes."

"Ssshh. I'm trying to think!" Geno answered.

"Think about what?"

"Hold on! I almost have it."

"You are so weird," said his sister as she headed back down the hall toward her bedroom.

"Aha! It's tape! Mom covered the sticky note with clear packing tape so it wouldn't get wet and would stick to the sink. Detective Geno solves the case!"

He started bowing and waving to an imaginary audience. "Thank you, thank you very much. I'll be here all week."

"You'd better not be in there all week! Hurry up, I have to fix my hair!"

Geno was so impressed with his mystery-solving skills that he didn't hear his sister come back to the door. Oops.

"Hold your horses. I'll be out in a second."

He grabbed a hand towel to mop up the mirror and was reminded of something. He had been so wrapped up in solving the great sink sticky note mystery that he'd not read the note.

"Hmmm, let's see why Mom would leave a note in the sink."

He bent over the sink and read, "That was NOT two minutes. Brush your teeth longer."

"Geno, I'm serious. Hurry up! I can't go to school looking like this."

Now his sister was pounding on the door. He opened the door to let her in, she pushed past him toward the mirror, and her smooth flip flops went sliding on the water-soaked floor. She hit the toilet with a thud. "Owww!" she hollered. "What in the world have you been doing in here? There's water everywhere!"

"Brushing my teeth," Geno answered.

"With what? A fireman's hose? Never mind, just move. Now I only have about two minutes to work a hair miracle."

"I always fix my hair in two minutes. You'll be fine," Geno assured her.

She made a noise at him, and furiously started spraying hairspray.

Geno picked up his toothbrush to start "Round 2."

"Yuck! This tastes like hairspray!"

"I thought you already brushed your teeth," his sister retorted.

"I did. Then I found another sticky note."

"Ohhhhhh. Say no more," she said sympathetically.

All of a sudden, his sister had gone from irritated to compassionate. She knew the power of the sticky notes too well. One thing was certain, although they didn't agree on everything, they did agree on one thing: Their mom was definitely sticky-note crazy. It was a private little laugh they shared, which brought them closer, for a moment, anyway.

Geno finished brushing at the same exact moment his sister finished her hair. "Done!" they both said in unison.

Geno and his sister laughed at their perfectly timed finish, as they headed toward the door for school.

"Remember to have a good day!" Geno's sister called out to him, as she got on her bus.

"I'll try, but I really wish I had a sticky note to remind me!" he hollered back.

She gave one big laugh and bounded up the bus steps, waving goodbye. He waved back and sat down on the curb to wait for his bus. Geno was so glad it was Friday. School was fine, but he loved going to church. It was the highlight of his week. *Only two more days,* he thought.

Geno finished up his school day but not without finding six more sticky notes. Usually on Fridays he found seven or eight, but his mom must have been busy. Which was "A-OK" with Geno, since every sticky note meant another job to do. Saturday came and went with its normal sticky note count of 14. He had created his own little game to keep track of his mom's sticky notes each day. Maybe that's why he was so good at math. Finally, it was time for bed and...teeth brushing. This time he knew exactly what the little piece of paper in the sink was and what it said. No cheating now. He endured a full two minutes of teeth-brushing torture. Oh well, the good news was that tomorrow was his favorite day of the week.

It was Communion Sunday, and Geno was looking at his Bible. There was a sticky note on the cover that said, "Don't forget me!"

Oh brother, he thought. *Even at church I can't seem to escape sticky notes!*

As the pastor talked, Geno opened his Bible to look for the story of the Last Supper. *I'm pretty sure he said Luke 22,* Geno thought to himself, as he turned the pages of his Bible as fast as he could.

Geno liked to see how fast he could find a scripture, even when no one else was racing him. When he found the place where Luke 22 was supposed to be, it wasn't there. His Bible skipped from Luke 21 right to Luke 23.

That's weird, thought Geno. *My Bible must be defective!*

Geno took a closer look. Something didn't seem quite right, and with his fingernail Geno picked at the edge of the page. There were two pages sticking together. After a minute the pages separated, revealing Luke 22.

"I gotcha!" Geno said out loud, without thinking about where he was.

A woman sitting in front of him turned around and gave him one of those grown-up looks.

"Not you, I meant Luke," explained Geno, feeling embarrassed.

The lady kept staring at him with a very unhappy expression.

"They were stuck," he whispered.

She gave him one last glare then turned around. When Geno looked down, he saw why Luke 22 had been stuck. A sticky note from his mom caused the pages to stick together. She wrote, "Don't ever forget what Jesus did, son. He gave His body and His blood for us. Read and remember."

Geno read the story in Luke 22. He closed his Bible as the pastor closed in prayer. Geno decided that Luke 22 was the best "sticky note" he had ever read!

THE END

Notes:

DAY 5: GAME TIME HULA-HOOP® THREAD

 Suggested Time: 5-8 minutes

 Memory Verse: This is my body which is given for you. Do this to remember me. –1 Corinthians 11:24

Supplies: ☐ 2 Hula Hoops®, ☐ Small prizes, ☐ Upbeat music to play during the game (optional)

(Corresponds with Lesson Outline No. I-II)

Game Instructions:

Divide players into 2 equal teams. Have each team stand in a straight line, side by side, and join hands. At no time during this activity can the players let go of their teammates' hands, or their team will be disqualified. Place a Hula Hoop® in the free hand of the player at the start of each line, so each team has a hoop. When the game begins, each player holding the Hula Hoop® will step through it and shift it to the next player, while continuing to hold hands. Continue passing the hoop until it reaches the end of the line.

The player at each end will step completely through the Hula Hoop® and hold it in his/her free hand. Once the hoop reaches the end, have each team send it back to the beginning of the line, using the same process. Players will have to use teamwork to keep the hoop from getting "stuck" along the line!

Game Goal:

The first team to send the Hula Hoop® down the line and back, wins!

Final Word:

This game is great for building friendships and learning to work together. Jesus loves friendship; in fact, one of the last things He did before dying on the cross was to have dinner with His closest friends!

Notes:_____

_____

_____

_____

_____

_____

_____

ACTIVITY PAGE

LAST SUPPER COLOR-BY-NUMBER

 Memory Verse: This is my body which is given for you. Do this to remember me. –1 Corinthians 11:24

(Corresponds with Lesson Outline No. II)

This week you studied about Jesus' Last Supper with His disciples. Now, color in this picture to reveal what special things He served at this meal.

0=WHITE
1=PURPLE
2=YELLOW
3=BROWN
4=PINK
5=BLACK
6=BLUE
7=GREEN
8=ORANGE

Notes _____

_____

_____

_____

_____

_____

_____

_____

_____

_____

_____

_____

_____

_____

_____

_____

_____

_____

_____

_____

_____

_____

_____

_____

_____

_____

_____

_____

_____

_____

_____

_____

_____

_____

_____

CPSIA information can be obtained at www.ICGtesting.com
Printed in the USA
LVOW02s1903241013

357975LV00003BC/7/P